TrustWorthy: New Angles On Trusts From Beneficiaries and Trustees

Hartley Goldstone and Kathy Wiseman

PRAISE FOR *TRUSTWORTHY*

This is the one book to read this year if you are creating your estate plan, if you are a trustee or a beneficiary, or if you advise families of wealth. You will not think about trusts in the same way again.

Charles W. Collier, Former Senior Philanthropic Advisor at Harvard University and author of *Wealth in Families*

TrustWorthy should be required reading not only for trustees and beneficiaries, but also for grantors and trusted family advisors. Hartley and Kathy's decision to use storytelling to reveal the vast potential in the trustee and beneficiary relationship was a stroke of genius. The stories in this book are inspiring and do a great job of demonstrating how trusts can be used not only to transfer financial wealth, but also to transfer legacy from one generation to the next.

Sara Hamilton, CEO and Founder, Family Office Exchange

TrustWorthy is must reading for any trust-creator, trustee or beneficiary who wants to improve their relationships and the effectiveness of the trust. Hartley and Kathy's greatest service — besides sharing their stories and tools for bringing about positive change — may be to refocus the attention of both trustees and beneficiaries on the fact that theirs is a relationship between human beings.

John P.C. Duncan, Kozusko Harris Duncan

Hartley Goldstone and Kathy Wiseman have given the participants in a "trustscape" (trust-creators, trustees and beneficiaries) an invaluable resource for creating the types of structures and relationships that will enable beneficiaries to see trust assets as life-affirming gifts and not burdens. Through the effective use of storytelling they have created the type of memorable models that help translate "legalese" into positive relationship-building action plans.

Lee Hausner, PhD., Managing Director of First Foundation Advisors and author of *Children of Paradise* and *The Legacy Family*

Hartley Goldstone and Kathy Wiseman help us understand that in spite of the negativity that seems all too pervasive in the world of trusts, there are many positive stories to be told about the interactions between trustees and the beneficiaries they serve. In **TrustWorthy***, you will find hope and a new vision.*

John A. Warnick, J.D., Founder of the Purposeful Planning Institute

Families with wealth often ask us, "What are other families doing?" With its wonderful collection of stories, **TrustWorthy** *provides some of the answers, and so helps family members turn trusts — which can seem so problematic and a source of stress — into positive opportunities for communication, education, and growth. This is a valuable resource for families who want to make thoughtful decisions regarding their trusts.*

Drs. Keith Whitaker and Susan Massenzio, Wise Counsel Research Associates and co-authors (along with James E. Hughes Jr.) of *The Cycle of the Gift*

TrustWorthy *is a must read for anyone having a role in a trust. The array of positive stories defies the lore that trusts are necessarily bad and burdensome. The reader will come away from these stories with hope and confidence in the power to shift to a better outcome, along with specific ideas to act upon to build strength in their families.*

Thayer Cheatham Willis, LCSW, Principal, Thayer Willis LLC and author of *Navigating the Dark Side of Wealth* **and** *Beyond Gold*

The relationship between a trustee and beneficiary is all too often fraught with tension more appropriate to competitors, rather than teammates pursuing a common goal. In their new book, Hartley Goldstone and Kathy Wiseman show how to harness the power of simple stories to achieve elegant, trustworthy results. This is important reading for all families of wealth.

Dirk Junge, Chairman and CEO of Pitcairn

*By viewing the beneficiary/trustee relationship from a qualitative perspective, Hartley and Kathy produce startling insights on virtually every page. Given the crucial importance of private capital in America's competitive success, and the fact that roughly 90% of that capital ends up in trust by the third generation, **TrustWorthy** makes a hugely important contribution — not just to trust-creators, trustees and beneficiaries, but to the nation as a whole. Best of all, Hartley and Kathy do it through stories and vignettes that are a delight to read: Simultaneously entertaining, moving, absorbing and inspiring.*

Gregory Curtis, Chairman and Founder of Greycourt & Co Inc. and author of *The Stewardship of Wealth*

*The collection of positive stories in **TrustWorthy** is compulsory reading for anyone in Asia who is a trust-creator, a beneficiary, or involved in any way with the trust industry. In traditional Asian culture, wealth-creators are obligated to leave family members functioning at a higher level — to leave successful flourishing families. **TrustWorthy** is squarely focused on the family system. The book is filled with role models and examples of how other families have used trust relationships to nurture mature, responsible beneficiaries. Reading the stories will change the way you think about trusts and how you select trustees, trust-protectors and advisors.*

Christian Stewart, Managing Director of Family Legacy Asia (HK) Limited, and former head of Wealth Advisory in Asia for JPMorgan Private Bank

*I want to thank Hartley and Kathy for bringing to life the undeniable, fundamental issues embedded in the trustee/beneficiary relationship that for so long have contributed to a breakdown in a family's systems. **TrustWorthy** is a must read, not only for advisors to families, but for each individual who already has, or will, set up, a trust. I recommend to each of our family clients that they read this book.*

Ken Polk, CEO, Arlington Family Offices

Kathy Wiseman and Hartley Goldstone have created an important and timely book that is sure to be deeply valuable for many. Their work is at once intimate and informative, thought-provoking and evocative. The reader is captivated at the beginning and stays that way throughout! Every grantor, beneficiary and trustee should consider this essential reading.

Ellen Miley Perry, Founder, Wealthbridge Partners and author of *A Wealth of Possibilities — Navigating Family, Money and Legacy*

Hartley and Kathy are advancing the conversation on this very important topic. Too many times have we seen beneficiaries and trustees stuck in an unproductive (and often adversarial) relationship, and too few times in a productive, mutually rewarding one. The potential for growth and empowerment for beneficiaries of a trust is huge, but so often goes untapped. The stories in **TrustWorthy** *demonstrate that potential, and we can all use them to inspire us (trust-creators, trustees and beneficiaries alike) to do better and achieve more.*

Scott A. Winget, Sr. Managing Director of Wealth Impact Planning, Ascent Private Capital Management of U.S. Bank

In writing **TrustWorthy**, *Hartley and Kathy have provided a wonderful guide for both beneficiaries and trustees who, to date, have had a scarcity of material to assist them.*

Anne D'Andrea, Co-founder and Executive Director of Collaboration for Family Flourishing

In **TrustWorthy**, *Hartley Goldstone and Kathy Wiseman have told a new story about the world of trusts — one that can inspire concerned parents, educate baffled children and guide well-intentioned trustees. Full of real life stories reflecting compassion and wisdom in the midst of complexity, this book demonstrates, once and for all, how trusts can go beyond merely enabling entitlement to empowering beneficiaries as they live deeply connected and purposeful lives. This is a must read for trust-creators, beneficiaries and trustees.*

Matthew Wesley, J.D., M.Div., Family Consultant

Hartley and Kathy, with great perception and compassion, have collected the "good" stories about how enriching a trust can be. The stories are thought-provoking and fun to read.

Barbara Hauser, J.D., author of *International Basic Guide to Trusts* **and** *International Family Governance*

Hartley Goldstone and Kathy Wiseman are making a huge contribution to the very challenging space of wealth management — the dilemma-filled world of trusts, trustees and beneficiaries. **TrustWorthy** *will be on the must read list for existing trust participants, as well as families and advisors contemplating wealth transfer strategies.*

G. Scott Budge, author of *The New Financial Advisor*

It is a well-documented fact that unsuccessful transitions of wealth between generations are the result of a lack of communication and trust, and a failure to prepare heirs. **TrustWorthy** *is groundbreaking work that every advisor needs to be familiar with when helping families and fiduciaries deal with these important issues.*

Eric D. Sanderson, Esq.

What a magnificent contribution! These elegant stories humanize the experience of being a trustee, a trust-creator, or a beneficiary. I can imagine in the future that **TrustWorthy** *will accompany every thoughtful trust document, and be a tattered, well-read book on the shelves of many great families.*

Peter A. Evans, Principal, aFgo Associates

As the old farmer said, "You sure know how to get the hay on the ground where the calves can get at it!"

A senior family member, self-described curmudgeon, trustee, and long-term observer of the high-net-worth-family world

DEDICATION

To the Storytellers — for their extraordinary courage and generosity.

And to Loyce, Ben and Jon for their unyielding love, support and patience while this book was being written.

— Hartley Goldstone

With deep appreciation for the relationships that encouraged and challenged my thinking. To Roslyn Gold Klaus and Morton Klaus for the legacy they provided. To Dr. Murray Bowen, Andrea Schara, Priscilla Friesen, John Engels, and Dan Papero, whose ideas make all the difference in my professional legacy. To my sisters Mary, Nancy and Peggy Klaus for our shared legacy as sisters. To my next generation Rosalind, James, Zack, Adriana and Zoe whose differences underscore the challenges of a legacy. To Elijah, Roane, Noah and Miss W who carry the legacy forward.

— Kathy Wiseman

CONTENTS

FOREWORD
by James E. Hughes Jr.

Imagine yourself in a conference room on the 30th floor of a New York City office building in the late 1980s. You have been invited to attend a meeting of people who are interested in understanding the nature of the relationship between a beneficiary and his or her trustee.

When you received this invitation, you wondered why you couldn't remember ever receiving anything similar. Then you wondered: "Even though I've been the beneficiary of a trust for 25 years, do I really have any idea about my relationship with my trustee, except that it has been passionless, a burden, and made me feel dependent?"

Finally you said to yourself: "Although I usually say no to invitations like this, I am intrigued. I will attend."

So here you are, in a room of 85 people, all looking strangely at one another. As you talk with each other, you discover that nearly all of them have had your same thoughts and experiences. Now you are really wondering: "What did I let myself in for when I accepted?" Or worse: "Oh my goodness. Am I in a support group for failed beneficiaries?!?"

At this point a nice young attorney, one whom you met some years ago and whose invitation it was that you had accepted, opens the meeting. He says: "I thank each of you for your courage in being here today and, by your attendance, convincing me that I was courageous [read: not crazy] for believing you would come. And also showing that you, as do I, have a desire to make your relationship with your trustee one that helps you flourish, be self-empowered, and free."

You say to yourself: "I am dumbfounded and delighted. I know why I came."

The same young attorney then advises that, for some years, he has been aware that nearly all families with significant financial wealth, by their third generation, hold some nine-tenths of that wealth in trust. He calls it a kind of "trust wave" caused by our tax laws and our fear of creditors.

He adds that for the past few years he has been in many rooms like this one, full of beneficiaries, and he always polls them, asking: "Is your trust a burden or a blessing?" Then he advises us that, in every room, 80% of the beneficiaries say: "A burden!!!"

And so, you discover that you're not alone, but rather part of a large majority of fellow sufferers. You see that what nearly everyone thinks must be the best thing on the planet — to get money throughout a lifetime without having earned it — is, for those who are beneficiaries, anything but. As this message is delivered, the room gets so pregnant with awakened silence that one could hear a pin drop.

It is at this meeting that you make a promise: "I will learn to be an excellent beneficiary and turn every effort toward making my relationship with my trustee one that helps me flourish."

But then — you can find nothing to read, no one willing to teach you, nor is your trustee interested in being your mentor.

I was the young attorney who actually convened that meeting. I invited 100 people, expecting 10 to 15 of those hundred to take part — and 85 showed up. I was stunned. I realized I wasn't wrong about what I was learning from the beneficiaries whom I had surveyed. I was learning that, if asked, beneficiaries will stand up and say: "I don't want to be rendered dependent by my trustee any more. I want my trustee to help me integrate the trust into my life, so that it makes me free to fulfill my dreams. I want to learn and practice what it means to be an excellent beneficiary."

Over the years since that meeting, I have been hoping that a service offered by great teachers would emerge to help beneficiaries and their trustees   deconstruct   and   reconstruct   their   beneficiary/trustee relationships to answer those deep calls for help quoted in the prior paragraph.

As I went looking for such teachers, I came to see that not only was the beneficiary/trustee relationship failing to function well in most families, but that many other relationships — what I call "we" relationships — were also entropic. Thus, their limited partnerships were failing for the lack of educated limited partners. Their corporations were failing for the lack of educated stewarding/conserving/stakeholder owners. Their philanthropies were failing for the lack of educated strategic philanthropists.

On and on, as I deconstructed why families weren't functioning in their "we" relationships, I came to the same conclusion: No one was teaching them how to make their legal "forms" function excellently. I found that their "form givers" (lawyers and other advisors) offered no instruction on how to make them function or, if they did, the instructions were incomprehensible except to the experts who wrote them and, I assume, to their peers. Certainly not to the users.

Observing the failure of these "we" relationships, I also discovered that, in many of these same families, their "me" relationships were not functioning well either. These are our relationships as sons, daughters, parents, grandparents, aunts, uncles, etc.

Once I could see that so many "we" and "me" relationships weren't functioning, I could also see why joint decision-making systems didn't work. Families assumed that their underlying relationships were functioning excellently, and they weren't.

I now understood why so many families fall prey to the "shirtsleeves to shirtsleeves in three generations" proverb that spells entropic doom. They could not make the positive decisions they needed to make to avoid the proverb's predicted outcome. Why? Because they weren't able to make their relationships work.

I also realized that it wasn't for lack of awareness, it was for lack of education.

3

It was then that I began to search for teachers who were interested in deconstructing each such relationship so it could be fully understood by the parties to it, and who would then help those parties reconstruct each relationship themselves, so it was sound and could function excellently.

It was on this journey to higher family functioning and flourishing that I discovered that two colleagues, Hartley Goldstone and Kathy Wiseman, were coming to exactly the same conclusion and that they had a particular interest in the beneficiary/trustee relationship. I urged them to consider deconstructing and reconstructing this relationship.

To my delight and to the good fortune of every beneficiary and trustee going forward, they took up the challenge to do just that and *TrustWorthy* is the magnificent result.

You, dear reader, are about to go on the positive journey that is the ongoing effort of Hartley and Kathy to reengineer the beneficiary/trustee relationship toward its higher functioning — functioning that leads to the beneficiary's independence, to helping bring dreams to life, and to achieving his or her highest self-awareness, self-empowerment, and full pursuit of happiness.

That Hartley and Kathy have chosen "positive story" as their medium to begin this process is brilliant. Story is what awakens imagination and helps us experience things in human terms. It is story that connects us to our innate humanity. It is in the stories of positive beneficiary/trustee relationships that we can most simply appreciate what "good relations" mean and which practices bring them about.

To change anything rooted in negativity (recall 80% of beneficiaries say their trustee relationship is a burden) needs heavy dynamite. The positive stories in this book are the gentle bomb that blows away that negativity, so that the positive gifts of trusts — as acts of generosity, magnanimity and love designed to enhance the lives of their beneficiaries — can again be the norm of beneficiary/trustee experience.

Thank you, Hartley and Kathy, for making my dream for the founders and beneficiaries of trusts — that their trusts be gifts of love and enhance their beneficiaries' lives — come true.

Namaste.

James (Jay) E. Hughes Jr.
Aspen, Colorado
August 2012

INTRODUCTION

This book is the product of two authors, an array of trusted storytellers, and much wise counsel.

By supplanting prevailing assumptions and behaviors, our objective is to transform the most complex, conflicted and difficult relationship known under the law — the "arranged marriage" between beneficiary and trustee.

Here's the big question: Can the widespread dissatisfaction, and all the talk of "problem" beneficiaries and "problem" trustees, give way to more creative and productive relationships?

We say: "Absolutely." And if your intuition is the same as ours, the harder question becomes "how do we get from here to there?" To help find out, we went to the source — beneficiaries, trustees and their advisors — and asked them for positive stories about moments in time when their relationships have worked well.

And those stories constitute the heart of *TrustWorthy*.

Hartley Goldstone and Kathy Wiseman
Denver, Colorado, and Washington D.C.
October 2012

CHAPTER ONE:
THE POSITIVE STORY PROJECT
by Hartley Goldstone

The year was 1989. My law firm split up and I accepted a senior trust-officer position with a regional bank. Despite having drafted trust instruments, I had little exposure to the landscapes they created for the succeeding generations.

On the first morning in this new role, I was handed roughly 25 files representing about 60 trusts — and it was like receiving a passport to new terrain. Over and again, I will see beneficiaries treating personal trusts as problems to be solved. A sampling…

- A soon to be 21-year-old had been orphaned at a very young age, his parents killed in a tragic car accident. Growing up, many of his expenses are paid from a trust holding substantial life-insurance proceeds. Upon turning 21, the trust will come to an end and he will receive a considerable sum. Might this approaching event add firmness and a real sense of future to his perspective? In this case, no, for he happens to be immature, showing little inclination to plan beyond his payday. He tries to game the system by creatively plotting to secure an early distribution to keep his "friends" around. Within a year following his 21st birthday, the money is gone, and so are the friends.

- A woman in her forties takes me aside at a conference. "My life is successful by almost any measure," she explains. "I am a tenured professor at an Ivy League university. I have a wonderful husband and children. I sit on several non-profit boards and currently chair my family's foundation. The only place that I am treated like a child is when I visit my trustee. I have come to terms with this, but my concern is that my children will have to go through the same thing."

- A distraught widow, mere days after losing her husband, is shocked to learn that her financial resources will be held in trust as a result of her late husband's tax planning. Our bank, as the trustee, is therefore an unexpected, and unwelcome, intrusion into her life.

Now and then, though, trusts are seen as opportunities to be embraced…

- The thirty-something beneficiary calls one day to say: "I've been living on checks from trusts my whole life without questioning where they come from or when they will end. I'm now doing my own estate planning and thinking about my children. I have no idea how the trusts that were set up for me will affect them. And so it's time for me to grow up, and really understand my trusts — can you help me?" This is the beginning of a conversation that will unfold over the coming months.

- A beneficiary is challenged with addictions for much of his adult life. The trust that his late grandfather created purchases a condominium for him, supports his basic needs and pays for a variety of treatment programs over the years. His father's heartbreak and frustration lead him to alternate among compassion, hostility and estrangement. Beneficiary, father and I have regular phone contact and occasional "crisis meetings." Son puts together sustained sobriety and other productive steps toward resurrecting his life. Father and son reconcile, and they include me in conversations about how the family's trusts can bring the larger family together.

- A recent college grad asks for help drafting her first business plan. Our conversation includes how the trust might support her dream and what would be required of her to receive financial backing. She does her homework and concludes that the idea is not sound. She goes back to the drawing board to start over again.

I was part of so many additional stories of people coming to terms, some more successfully than others, with the trusts that they live with. Imagine the effect of these snapshots and discoveries over more than two decades — for it's this perspective that has led directly to my current work, including the creation of this book.

During a decade of administering trusts — and then another decade helping families plan for their next generations — I went heedlessly along, then uneasily along, and then — BAM! The cumulative effect of years of trust-related encounters collided with the rich teachings of a newly met mentor. (More about that person soon.) It was the shock of realization, followed by the thrill of being introduced to a like-minded community.

As a result, my beliefs had to change, and they did: I now define the "trustscape" — by which I mean a subsystem of the larger family system populated by those touched by the family's trusts — as a realm where opportunities transcend problems.

And so — here's where I stand today:

1. Like everyone else, beneficiaries and trustees create stories to put a given moment into context. Sometimes the story is a detailed "narrative," other times it's a "slant" or "spin," but in any case the story becomes their reality. The story might serve them well, or not so well. The point is the ability to direct the thinking: Beneficiaries and trustees can decide upon their point of view — trusts as a problem, or trusts as an opportunity.

2. Many lawyers and trustees emphasize the quantitative (law, investment, tax, administration) and downplay the qualitative (intrapersonal and interpersonal). Maybe that's fine for beneficiaries who require little more than a transactional relationship. For most, though, it will lead to trouble.

    Whether it's a trust-creator speaking with his lawyer, or a beneficiary making inquiries to her trustee, the message is some form of "I hope you can provide what I need." Too often, the response back — without using these words, of course — amounts to "I hope you need what I can provide." And the disconnect happens mostly because quantitative skills differ in profound ways from the qualitative ones.

Some lifelong trustscape observers emphasize qualitative over quantitative in a ratio somewhere north of three-to-one. I agree with them. You cannot expect to have an exemplary trustscape anchored in quantitative outcomes alone — no matter how good those outcomes are. It's spending a sufficient amount of time and energy on qualitative matters that brings about flourishing trustscapes.

3. Under stress, a trustscape system, like any social system, can be changed for the better in a number of ways. I'll mention two: Fix what's gone wrong, or build upon what's going right. The former — traditional problem-solving — looks to reduce breakdowns and make repairs in order to reach an "acceptable" state. I adhere to the latter approach: Figure out what's going right (while also acknowledging any difficulties); build upon that positive core; and set the group's sights on arriving at an exceptional trustscape that goes well beyond acceptable.

My approach can be summed up as: Getting the most out of personal trust relationships by surfacing and building upon unexplored potentials.

Sounds nice, but — how to begin? Trustscapers should listen to each other's stories about peak moments where the best in them has been touched.

COMING TO TERMS WITH TERMS (AND PROCEDURES)

The trust concept originated during the time of the Crusades. English knights went off to war knowing that they would be gone for a long time and might not survive to return home. So the knight asked someone he trusted — quite often it would be the bishop — to look after his property. The knight instructed his trustee on how to manage the property and what to do with the property should word get back that he had died.

The nature of trusts — someone transfers property to someone else to manage on behalf of someone — hasn't changed much over the years.

The person who creates a trust often goes by names such as "grantor" or "settlor." We'll go with **trust-creator**, a term suggested by my friend John A. Warnick. And a **trustee** — one entrusted — is today defined as "one put in charge of another's property." Completing the loop, the person who benefits is, of course, the **beneficiary**.

The trustee is legal owner of property held by the trust. The trustee has a **fiduciary duty** to ignore his own interests and administer the property for the benefit of the beneficiary. In this way, the beneficiary obtains use of the property without being its technical owner.

The **will** or **trust agreement** that creates the trust is more or less a set of instructions from the trust-creator: Who are the players? What property will be governed by the trust agreement? How is the property to be managed? When shall the trustee make distributions of **principal** (property of the trust) or **income** (income generated by the property such as interest, dividends, or rent)? When will the trust end and what happens to the property?

An enlightened trust-creator will communicate his or her intent, along with hopes, dreams and blessings. Much more about that later, indeed throughout the rest of this book.

Family systems theory (which co-author Wiseman will speak more about in Chapter Two) is a body of ideas that is surprisingly pertinent to trust relationships. Our term **trustscape** describes a subsystem within the larger family system. Members of the trustscape are those connected by a trust agreement — trust-creators, trustees, beneficiaries, trust-protectors, committees and their advisors.

We liken the trustscape to a seascape. Both have currents and crosscurrents on the surface and below. Some days are sunny with clear sailing. On other days, fog rolls in and squalls unexpectedly arise. Navigating either "scape" is at times enchanting and at other times hazardous.

Now let's shift from nomenclature to the trust administration process. Settling in as a trust officer in 1989, I had dozens of trusts to administer. My immediate team included an investment portfolio manager and my assistant. Centralized departments monitored specialized assets such as real estate, oil and gas interests and insurance policies owned by the trusts. Our tax department saw to tax-compliance and reporting. An operations group prepared internal reports and statements.

Most of the correspondence was from beneficiaries requesting funds. The decision whether to honor a request involved several steps. The threshold question was, "Is the request allowable under terms of the trust?"

Then we'd go on to consider the reasonableness of the request, the beneficiary's history of requests, the size of the request as compared to the size of the trust, the impact on the trust's ability to serve other beneficiaries, and so forth.

I had authority to approve or deny requests up to a certain dollar limit. If the amount exceeded my authority, I presented the request along with my recommendation to a distribution committee that met weekly. The committee was comprised of senior trust officers. I took my turn chairing the committee.

Legal skills obviously came in handy. But I was also glad for the time spent — this was before law school — on the staff of a social-services agency. The experience of assisting people sort through challenges, which could be full-blown crises, came in handy. It was a daily effort to square the language of trust instruments with the life situations of beneficiaries.

Over the next 10 years the bank grew to become a very large and diverse financial institution through a series of mergers. With each merger came more stringent policies and procedures. On some days I felt like a paper-pusher — someone who needed a new approach, and especially more operational freedom, to avoid letting our trust clients down.

One day in 1999, a call came in that was an invitation to join a small team. The team's mandate was to design a multi-family office for the bank's wealthiest families — dynastic families with complex issues. I jumped at the chance. Within a short time, our staff grew to include a couple of psychologists and a family historian, in addition to the usual legal, investment, insurance, accounting, trust and banking professionals.

I stayed on as a planner for clients of the multi-family office for another decade. Then, in September 2009, I left the corporate world to establish Trustscape LLC — a firm for maximizing trust relationships through speaking, writing, consulting and coaching.

BREAKING DOWN WHY IT BREAKS DOWN

Too many estate plans fail succeeding generations and the trustees that serve them. Here are some reasons for the troublesome outcomes (while acknowledging readers whose trustscapes are the sterling exception):

The Trust-Creator. The attorney, accountant, investment advisor, and insurance professional — call them the nucleus of the advisory team — are well-versed in technical matters. So estate plans are usually pretty good at preserving assets in a tax-efficient manner while providing for distributions to family members, charitable institutions, and perhaps others.

What's often missing is deliberation about the plan's impact on the long-term sustainability of the family (as opposed to sustainability of the family's financial assets). Scant attention is paid to whether the trusts, as written, will be a positive force at all stages of loved ones' lives.

The outcomes are predictable. And, without a doubt, if trust-creators could glimpse their plans playing out, time and again we'd hear about "trust-creator's remorse."

The Beneficiary. Beneficiaries most often enter the relationship with their trustees with little or no explanation or training. Education typically consists of informal meetings where the trustee or the attorney explains how the trust works and the portfolio manager talks about investments.

Understanding how the trust works and a basic knowledge of investments are important to a beneficiary, but do not address the fundamental issue: Successfully integrating the trust into his or her life.

The Trustee. Trust professionals are usually sound at managing quantitative aspects of trusts — legal, tax, investing, and administration. Regulatory oversight and the threat of litigation are facts of life, so as you would expect, there's an emphasis on risk-management — especially when it comes to the quantitative. This approach too often becomes a self-filling prophecy if it ignores qualitative issues like whether the method of trust administration heightens beneficiaries' lives.

Family-member trustees have additional concerns. Being a trustee can be time-consuming and personally challenging, often requiring dedication to service well beyond doing what's easy.

And, if I could share a story, it would center on a time and place long before being invited to administer trusts. Though bank experience was a sustained introduction to the trustscape, my family was no stranger to a failed wealth-transfer.

My father's father came to this country — alone, at the age of 15 — around the time the 19th century gave way to the 20th. "Grandpa" Nathan built a business that bought steel from the mills and cut, riveted and welded the steel for construction projects in and around New York City.

Growing up, I was proud to cross the George Washington Bridge or visit Yankee Stadium, Lincoln Center or later the World Trade Center Towers knowing that we had steel in each. Perhaps most awe-inspiring was the day — I must have been five or so — that my father took me to see a brand new hospital wing where a plaque honored Grandpa and my grandmother "Mama Jeane."

My father, as the oldest son, was heir apparent to the steel business. Some of my favorite memories were going to work with him. Visiting the office was like a family reunion. But the real action was in the yard below. The noise was deafening and sparks flew everywhere. Overhead cranes unloaded steel beams and columns that arrived on enormous trucks. Huge saws and torches cut the steel to size. Red-hot rivets were pounded into place. Joints were welded. Fabricated steel was loaded onto other trucks for delivery to construction sites.

It didn't get any better for a child dreaming of working there one day.

But that was not to be. The business failed around the time of Grandpa's death in 1966. Fallout from settlement of his estate ate up most of the remaining assets and splintered our family. The "emotional cutoff" between my father and his sisters was swift and severe — they never spoke again. Aunts, uncles and cousins that I had grown up with would no longer be part of my life.

This had a powerful impact: It left with me with a firsthand sense of how inter-generational wealth issues can affect a family.

So, what can be done? Trust-creators, trustees, beneficiaries and advisors can make a deliberate effort to pay attention to qualitative issues at every step — going all-out to maintain a three-to-one or better qualitative-over-quantitative ratio. Models are around if you look for them, in part because some families have been emphasizing the qualitative with increasing sophistication for generations. What's more, this book's collection of stories is a good place to start your search.

WITHIN REACH OF A NEW APPROACH

In my later corporate years, the qualitative side of multi-generational wealth grew more and more compelling. As so often happens when questioning one's underlying ideas, I met people who forever changed my thinking — especially about new approaches to trust relationships.

Here's a closer look at two guides who gave depth and method to the changes.

It would not be possible for me to overstate Jay Hughes' generosity and influence on my work. For starters, he taught me that families have three systems of capital — human, intellectual and financial — that have to be managed excellently for the successful trajectory of a family across generations. And success begins with quality joint decision-making.

Recall Jay's Foreword. He talked about the failure of family decision-making systems as a direct result of the failure of interpersonal relationships. Seen that way, the breakdown of the beneficiary/trustee relationship is a symptom of a larger problem. So if we learn to successfully "deconstruct and reconstruct" the relationship between beneficiaries and trustees, we may have a model for changing other relationships for the better, as well.

That's where the vital "three to one" ratio of qualitative to quantitative comes in. Relationships fall squarely on the "qualitative" side of the analysis of successful families. Jay first explained the ratio to me in metaphorical terms — how, in the world of chemistry, so often three measures of one element combine with one measure of a second to create a new compound that is stronger than either.

Jay and I continue to exchange ideas about how to bring favorable ratios into being, now with the benefit of innovative research being done in the rapidly developing field of "positive" psychology — the empirical study of optimal human functioning at the individual, group, and societal levels.

Positive psychologists have much to say about three-to-one (and higher) ratios of positive to negative interactions. The ratio has been shown to correlate with high performance, life satisfaction, and other measures of flourishing. (See "Notes, Sources, and Resources" at the end of this book.)

Now Guide #2: Jackie Kelm — not formally part of the trustscape — knows how to create positive change within social systems. She says to begin by paying attention to what we want more of, instead of dwelling on pathologies and other problems. Jackie is a corporate consultant who, among others, has pioneered the development and use of an exciting approach — Appreciative Inquiry. And the best way I know to illustrate "AI" is through a story told by Jackie.

The Cleveland Clinic is ranked by *U.S. News & World Report* as among our country's top hospitals. During the 1980s, the Clinic bought an adjoining hotel for the purpose of housing families of out-of-state patients. Since the hotel had been low-budget, money was spent to refurbish the rooms, lobby and so forth.

But the hotel's management continued to operate the way they had previously — as if the hotel were still low-budget. Management of the Cleveland Clinic asked for help from Case Western Reserve University's Weatherhead School of Management.

A brilliant PhD candidate, David Cooperrider, suggested the following: Send all of the hotel's employees, from housekeeping staff to senior management, to a five-star hotel in Chicago for a week.

The instruction: Interview the five-star staff and carefully observe and make note of everything done well during the week. At the conclusion, prepare a report of what was learned.

Do you sense the marked difference from the usual problem-solving method? The latter would likely have resulted in recommendations such as "replace the hotel's management" or, at the least, offer training — after, of course, showing the staff all that was not right in terms of efficiency, decor, and professionalism.

But the Cleveland Clinic went along with the Weatherhead School's different approach. Their hotel's employees went to Chicago for a week. And it paid off big-time.

Not too long after they returned, the former low-budget hotel was awarded a four-star rating. This was the first AI "intervention" — the first change agenda served by a conscious method of asking questions and interacting with examples that look likely to encourage self-directed excellence.

Today AI has evolved into a disciplined and robust approach to positive systems change taken up by major corporations, governmental entities, non-profits — the list goes on. While a full discussion of AI is well beyond the scope of this book, among its operating premises are: (1) We create stories about what we see; (2) the good, the bad, and everything in between may be found in every situation; and (3) the stories we create become our reality and we act accordingly.

You'll find more about Jay Hughes, Jackie Kelm and a few other influencers in "Notes, Sources, and Resources." Largely because of them, as mentioned earlier, my approach can be summarized as: Getting the most out of trust relationships by surfacing and building upon unexplored potentials.

In 2010, at Jay's suggestion, Kathy Wiseman and I began a conversation about combining our respective expertise and experience. For 30 years, Kathy has helped multigenerational families make important decisions arising from family business transitions. She teaches, writes and speaks extensively about family systems, and has used storytelling for years.

At first, Kathy and I wondered how we might collaborate. We spoke with different voices coming from diverse experience and points of reference. But it didn't take long to realize why Jay introduced us.

Our conversations led Kathy and me to develop "family trustscape meetings" — a way to engage members of a family's trustscape in conversations about the opportunities, constraints and challenges of their respective roles. This is a new approach that leads to stronger relationships and aligned expectations, with a secondary benefit of holding down the number of families involved in trust-litigation.

Subsequent conversations led to the design of workshops and education programs for beneficiaries and trustees. Meanwhile, my coaching practice gained traction. To our knowledge, no one other than Trustscape LLC is systematically applying elements of appreciative inquiry, positive psychology, and family systems theory to the trustscape.

FROM THE BIG PICTURE TO *TRUSTWORTHY*

TrustWorthy has its roots in The Beneficiary & Trustee Positive Story Project, begun in 2010. The thinking is that an effective way to optimize the beneficiary and trustee relationship is to hear stories that reveal strengths of the beneficiary, the trustee, and their relationship.

That is not to say that a given beneficiary/trustee relationship is working well all of the time or even most of the time. All human relationships have their ups and downs — we're interested in stories about the "up" times or that have led to "up" times. The Project is a quest for stories about concrete moments in time when relationships between beneficiaries and trustees are at their best.

Beneficiaries, trustees and their advisors have enthusiastically supported the Project. They have generously shared (and continue to share) stories with us. The heart of *TrustWorthy* is 25 of those stories, and the stars of this book are the storytellers.

We left out some names and facts and changed others to protect confidentiality, but each story comes from a beneficiary, trustee or advisor whose integrity and professionalism one or both authors can vouch for.

And we need to stress: The stories that comprise the bulk of this book are not composites, nor are they fictional. These are real stories generated from first-hand experiences that a friend might share over a cup of coffee.

Each story contains its own wisdom. When things are going well, what are beneficiaries and trustees saying? What are they doing? What circumstances contribute to breakthroughs and effective behaviors?

Please engage with these stories. Feed on the storytellers' experiences and take full advantage of their insights. Feel free to browse, move in and out, jump around. When a story is failing to grab you, pass it by. Find the people and themes that you connect with.

AN INVITATION TO JOIN IN

The Beneficiary & Trustee Positive Story Project is accelerating. We regularly post new stories beyond those in this book, along with related commentary, on our website NavigatingTheTrustscape.com.

We invite you to contribute a story or two. Help us deepen our understanding of flourishing trustscape relationships, illuminate best practices, develop practical applications — and we'll make the results broadly available.

For further information, email Hartley Goldstone at Hartley@NavigatingTheTrustscape.com. We treat all inquiries in confidence.

FOR BENEFICIARIES IN SEARCH OF MAJOR CHANGE

My first attempt to combine what I was learning from Jay and what I was learning about appreciative inquiry and positive psychology was a 2007 paper *On Becoming an Excellent Trust Beneficiary*. In it, I outlined a three-pronged approach for beneficiaries to re-position their trusts from being burdens, to being resources.

The beneficiary's first and most concrete task is to understand basic "quantitative" information — the language of the trust agreement, the relevant law, the trust statement, and the trustee's policies and procedures. Next, the beneficiary will learn how to build a positive relationship with his or her trustee. And finally, the beneficiary will come to view his or her trust as a gift in support of the journey toward a fulfilling, productive, meaningful life.

On Becoming An Excellent Trust Beneficiary can be downloaded without charge by visiting our website at NavigatingTheTrustscape.com.

CHAPTER TWO:
ESTATES & TRUSTS – THE HUMAN FACTOR
by Kathy Wiseman

The American Bar Association has said that one of the fastest growing areas of legal conflict and court proceedings is trust litigation. Reports of conflict among trustees and beneficiaries are common, making families and trust-managers alike ever more cautious about the design and administration of a trust.

But it does not have to be that way. This chapter maintains that trusts can assist people to "grow up," manage their trust and family relationships more effectively, and prevent significant conflict.

To "grow up" is part of the aging process yet not guaranteed by it. And, for parents and interested members of the extended family, the opportunity to "nurture" does not stop once the initial caretaking is finished.

The creation and administration of trusts, and passing of wealth from one generation to the next, goes well beyond managing money by astute tax and investment planning. Passing wealth on offers a twofold opportunity for both the trust-creator and beneficiary. It is the opportunity to provide another form of "nurturing." First, it has the potential to educate the next generation on the facts of living a fiscally sound life. Second, it is a unique and significant opportunity to promote maturity and a more defined "sense of self" in the beneficiary.

The relationship challenges that often lead to conflict — those that are inherent to trusts — have potential solutions that flow easily from knowledge of family systems. This approach can enhance maturity for a beneficiary; increase the "job satisfaction" of a trustee; and realize the thoughtful intentions of the trust-creator. (Please see the box at end of this chapter for my four-point explanation of maturity.) Additionally, it only takes one person — a family member, or a professional who is able to "think systems" — to help a family become more mature and thoughtful.

To become "mature" is to become a competent and responsible adult. It takes repeated attempts, here and there, as either crisis or opportunity allows, to take responsibility for one's own life while also functioning productively within social groups — family, community, school, physical and social environments. What is appropriate for one time and setting can be "overkill" in another. Administering a trust, as the beneficiary and the trustee age, is part of the challenge of excellent trust administration.

This next segment is about what a trust-creator can or cannot do. But trustees and especially beneficiaries will do well to "eavesdrop."

BEYOND THE FINANCIALS

My father was an estates-and-trusts attorney working in Philadelphia and counseling couples on passing their resources to the next generation. He earned his undergraduate and law degrees at the same time, completing them in his early twenties. He went on to practice for 40 years in a large Philadelphia law firm, of which he was a founding partner.

When he chose trustees and executors for his four daughters who were his only heirs (our mother died when we girls ranged in age from 9 to 18), his traditional training and caution "blinded" him. He did not see what eventually can create the real problems or opportunities — the "human" or "emotional" side of trusts and estates.

Dad's death at age 65 was sudden. His four daughters ranged in age from 18 to 29. On reaching adulthood we, as beneficiaries, needed an advisor who would teach, guide, mentor, and educate us. Vital choices for our daily life could not be grasped by absorbing the fine print of our father's estate documents. We needed trustees who could help us grow up. In so doing, they would need to develop a relationship with us that would preempt fatal differences of opinion, personal conflicts and litigation.

To manage the financial assets and legal requirements of the estate, Dad had chosen trustees and executors in whom he had confidence. He selected two men, one his law partner whom we did not particularly like, and my older cousin, a shy and introverted legal scholar. Since neither trustee had children, it was a mismatch from the start.

Different trustees could have helped us make decisions — such as the percentage of income to save, what to consider in buying a home, the implications of investing in our spouses' businesses, whether it is wise to lend money to family members, and how best to pay for education to advance our careers. While each decision had a financial element, each also had a "relationship" or human component that required consideration and encouraged the beneficiaries to think.

My parents' financial resources were only one of their legacies to us. They did communicate values and a strong code about the importance of family relationships. As sisters, the four of us are resources to each other.

However, our parents missed an opportunity. In both their planning process and in the creation of the trusts, they could have passed on to us their thinking about what to do financially to live a successful life and how to think about the kinds of issues noted above. We were left unprepared to use our experience as inheritors to learn and grow in our ability to make decisions alone and together.

The stories collected in this volume are not smooth or strife-free, but they are productive and enlightening. The dark side always gives way to the light. Be prepared for examples of trust administration processes that are both rigorous and flexible as they head in the direction of more maturity.

SEEING THE FAMILY AS AN EMOTIONAL UNIT

When Jay Hughes engineered my "professional blind date" with Hartley Goldstone, he encouraged me to bring my knowledge and experience with Family Systems Theory to Hartley's recently launched Positive Story Project. This section sums up that experience.

After obtaining an MBA and consulting to manufacturing, retail, social-service and not-for-profit enterprises, I was struck by how human or relationship issues slowed or blocked the implementation of strategic plans, goals, and business decisions. Individuals meant well, were well-educated, but stopped short. Why? They described the problem as "difficult people," "differences of opinion," "perceived threats" and "resistance to change," some mix of which had escalated anxiety and brought progress to a halt.

Such explanations were usually accurate, but never the whole truth. What was happening beneath the surface? In 1985, to explore such dynamics, I began to study with Dr. Murray Bowen, founder of the Georgetown University Family Center.

In Bowen's framework, popularly known as Family Systems Theory or Bowen Systems Theory, I found an approach to human behavior rooted in science. It was not blame-oriented and avoided "diagnosing dysfunction" in individuals — either within a family, or inside an organization. Instead, Bowen's focus was on the reciprocal interactions of individuals and family members (the influence each had on the other), in the present and over many generations, and the importance of thinking neutrally about the human condition in all its forms.

"Family systems" is a way to describe how the early relationships shape other relationships, especially our predictable responses under stress.

The focus of the theory is that one person can make a difference. One individual who decides to take more responsibility for him- or herself and their own reactions is key. If one person can relate neutrally and "think systems," during an intense human interaction, over time all parties will take more responsibility for their own views and actions and operate from a greater sense of maturity.

Bowen's groundbreaking research with schizophrenic families was the genesis of the idea of the family as an emotional unit. His thinking offers a way to look at the human, emotional side of family organizations in the first instance, and the management of trusts and estates now.

Three ideas are essential to thinking about the family as an emotional unit:

1. Whatever affects one family member affects the others as well, although the result might not look or sound the same in each individual. Anxiety is part of all life and is contagiously moving from one person to another. When parents do not address the difficulties they are having in their own lives, the next generation will be vulnerable — because what affects a family member during one generation has impact on the following generations.

2. Each family member adapts to the family relationship structure, exchanging "self" (or "giving in," for example) in order to keep the family stabilized. This is not usually a conscious effort. There are observable ways that individual members of a family respond to each other and to significant events. Knowing these patterns for yourself allows you to interrupt automatic actions, both in the family and at work. One observable process is that of the emotional triangle where problems between two people get moved to a third, reducing the stress of the original two.

3. Considering the family as an emotional unit, not a collection of autonomous individuals, changes everything about how you think about the family, the individual, and the responses of each to challenge and change. One cannot just look at the individual and hope to understand that person without understanding family or system relationships (past and present) that he or she is a part of.

Whether or not the trust-creator or beneficiary — to name just two — are aware of it, family relationships and their history are embedded in trusts. And any "problems" in the relationships in the family are likely to be reflected in the thinking that guides the design and administration of trusts. The lack of clarity of intention between the trust-creator and beneficiary — a father and his children, for example — may spill over into the beneficiary/trustee relationship.

Let's say the father creates a trust for the benefit of his children when his children are very young. He includes language in the trust instrument to mitigate what he sees as the "irresponsibility" or "poor work ethic" in his family; he does this based on experience with his own brothers and sisters from the past. Although his children are very young, the father includes them — and perhaps even the future generations — in this view.

But the father never tells his children — or for that matter the selected trustee — what the thinking, intentions and context were in creating that trust. By the time the children (now much older) inherit money, there is potential for conflict between the trustee and these beneficiaries. This is because the language mitigating "irresponsibility" and "poor work ethic" was based in the father's past — between the father and his siblings. Yet, it is lived as though it exists in the present with the beneficiaries.

That's one example of how a family, linked by a trust, creates hurdles and detours that stretch well beyond the lifespan of the trust-creator. Such situations lead to costly and drawn-out legal proceedings. Why? The legal proceedings are a substitute forum for what would have been better discussed at the family dinner table, family vacation or family meeting — all of which offer opportunities for relating directly and with transparency. These hurdles and challenges can be further compounded by a trustee's concern about liability in carrying out his or her fiduciary responsibility.

THE BEAUTY OF A TRIANGLE

Family Systems Theory describes the smallest unit of the emotional system as the triangle. This observable process helps us grasp what becomes problematic in family trusts.

When things are calm, two people can have open and direct communication and contact with one another. Introduce change, whether positive or negative — the birth of a child, the death of a parent, an increase or decrease in wealth, opening of a new division or the closing of a failing one — and the existing openness can quickly shift to anxiety and fear. Instead of relating directly among themselves, the two-party system reaches for a third to off-load the change, imbalance or upset.

In families and trusts, much can be understood in terms of how the triangle works. Trustees are often the third part of the triangle between the trust-creator and the beneficiary, making that role a critical one. One can help find solutions to the original contentious challenges by knowing the history of family relationships and how to be a third arm of a triangle, effectively relating to both sides of an issue. Staying in good contact with the different points of view, even when the differences become emotional, and knowing the part that one plays in the interaction are ways to manage oneself in a triangle.

Consider the trustee in the story that begins Chapter Four. In "The Seven-Year Struggle," this trustee walks along with a beneficiary who had injured another in a bar brawl. Advising from a third-party position, he was neither too distant nor too helpful. He navigated both sides of that triangle — in this case, the beneficiary and the legal system — in a way that allowed the responsibility to remain with the beneficiary.

Viewing families as "emotional units" of intricately connected individuals leads to certain best practices. Learning the facts of a family's history before a trust is created — who was important and who was more peripheral — can support maturity in individual family members.

Knowing the historical internal and external events that shaped the creator of the trust, and the relationships that shaped his or her thinking about passing on accumulated assets, adds to understanding.

LESS DEPENDENCE ON THE FAMILY FOR SELF-WORTH

In Bowen's framework, "defining a self" is the phrase used for the dynamic process of living in a family and having the ability to maintain a separate sense of self — even when anxiety is high and pressures abound to adapt in order to restore equilibrium in the system. It is a way to describe emotional maturity.

Increased independence and self-management are fundamental to maturity. Defining a self includes being able to set and reach one's own goals in spite of shifting circumstances. It reflects the ability to manage one's own disappointment, regulate one's own emotions, and persevere in the face of difficulties without blaming others. It is the ability to face difficult people and difficult circumstances without feeling threatened and running away.

A better-defined individual knows when he or she is acting impulsively to relieve the anxiety of the moment rather than tolerating it, acting thoughtfully and staying on course.

The process of defining a self is related directly to trust creation and trust administration. Writing and administering trusts based on promoting and maintaining rising levels of autonomy frees all parties from the paralyzing effects of controlling and second-guessing the behavior of another.

I suggest that the one of the primary goals of trust administration be the raising the next generation from dependence to interdependence to independence — that is, to support mature self-sufficient adults who produce mature, self-sufficient offspring. Complete independence is never achieved. The goal, however, is the attainment of a level of self-sufficiency and autonomy while remaining connected to family.

Achieving "self" can be particularly difficult under two circumstances: (1) When unearned income is provided and that unearned income is the sole or primary source of support for the next generation; and (2), when the parents or grandparents of adult beneficiaries — primarily for their own well-being — require the younger generation's emotional dependence on them. This "over-dependence" or "reliance," requiring the participation of both generations, makes self-sufficiency difficult.

An example would be when there is discord in a marriage and the spouses focus their attention and worry on the next generation, rather than dealing with the issues themselves. This "over-focus" on and "triangling" of the children into the parents' conflict often results in parents thinking that their kids are less capable than those kids in fact are. They may mistakenly conclude that their children cannot manage money, need support in making life decisions, and require constant monitoring. The children's unintended dependence and actions to satisfy their parents' needs are "out of the awareness" of both parents and children.

With such a process operating, trusts may be created that are overly focused on how to control the beneficiaries rather than on how to promote self-sufficiency.

BETTER LATE THAN NEVER: HOW MORT MET MURRAY

I wish that Dad, a no-nonsense kind of guy, and we four daughters as well, had the benefit of Dr. Bowen's thinking as Dad was writing his will and establishing his Trust. One of the challenges of trusts is that they do what they are fundamentally intended to do. They provide income from one generation in a family to another and they do it efficiently.

But efficiency is not necessarily effectiveness in the long run. Unearned income going to a beneficiary can impair his or her ability to take responsibility — to be a self. Because a beneficiary has not gotten the financial rewards due to his own effort but rather through the randomness of birth, a sense of accomplishment is denied. We have all seen instances in which unearned income impedes an individual's development of self-sufficiency and maturity.

Trust income often provides quick financial fixes to life's large and small challenges. This income does not necessarily provide the opportunity for the trust-creator or the beneficiary to engage in the real work of solving life's problems and/or growing up, as described above. It limits the "real-time education" that is a part of taking responsibility for one's self and one's actions and gaining a sense of competency.

One part of this evolution toward competency is learning about investing, philanthropy, life-planning, and advisor-selection. All are important to know and many families seek this kind of educational assistance. However, the second and most critical part of "education" hides below the surface and is learned over time — the beneficiaries' knowledge about themselves and their relationships. This knowledge, which has a substantial effect both on the individual and on the functioning of a trust, is often a missing piece in trust administration.

Considering trust creation and administration as an opportunity for greater maturity, one asks a different set of questions. Is it possible to receive unearned income and still be held accountable for one's life lessons you'll see described in several of the stories? Is it possible to understand where trust-creator control originated and how to think about it as a family process? With knowledge of a family over the generations, it is possible to structure a relationship with a trustee that promotes self-responsibility. This is where Dr. Murray Bowen could have enlightened my father, Morton Saul Klaus, Esq.

Imagine what my father might have done had he understood the human side of estates and trusts and the parental role in the promotion of maturity:

First, he could have shared with us more of his life experience and what he learned as the youngest in a family of six, as a soldier in World War II, and as a professional advisor who worked with many affluent families. This information would have given us a deeper and more personal understanding of what informed his thinking. My guess is that he planned to tell us much of this when he "got older." Unfortunately, he died sooner than he had planned.

Second, he could have provided us with a family-wealth "playbook" that addressed the decisions my sisters and I would have to make as beneficiaries, both individually and as a sibling group. For the four of us he could have described his principles of saving, spending and investing, and how making financial mistakes can ironically promote self-confidence and competence. Doing so would have helped us to know his thoughts on how to settle conflicts with his second wife, his law partners, and among us sisters. He might have offered thought-provoking questions and challenges for us to consider.

<u>Third</u>, it would have been helpful for him to suggest to us how we manage the relationships that are a part of being a trust beneficiary. Should we consider the trustee as a mentor or merely a cashier? Should we consider the money from the trust as part of our marital resources and share it with our spouse? What is it that we, his four daughters, might encounter as beneficiaries? How should we work with the trustees and what should we expect from them? How might we settle differences with them? How could we use the inherited resources to support our long-term goals rather than solving short-term crises?

Sharing that information, and those perspectives, and then eliciting ours, would have given us a chance to know our father better, talk about what the future might hold without him, and help us determine our own point of view.

THE VALUE OF POSITIVE STORIES

I believe that the anxiety reflected in the creation of and/or administration of trusts has to do with four basic relationship challenges that fall into four general categories: (1) The desire and determination to control or shape another's behavior; (2) not knowing the details of another's life experience and family history so that distance, disconnect and conflict occur; (3) behaving as though when someone disagrees with you, something is "wrong" with them rather than seeing it as a mutually created problem in the family system; and (4) the premise that cutting off and deciding "this relationship is not worth continuing" will solve the problem.

Working with families making decisions about the future and their assets, I speak with individuals who eagerly and actively engage in planning for their future and that of the family. But some family members are not particularly eager to think about these issues. At one-on-one or family meetings, they show up disinterested and "roll their eyes" in annoyance and boredom. They are not engaged in their family legacy and wealth-transfer. Do they think they are not deserving of the unearned income? Do they know how to manage the assets? Are they concerned about not having the intellectual wherewithal to participate in the major decisions?

The right stories, however, begin to engage these "eye-rollers." A good story is a personalized example — while not as "thick" as a case study, it does show how thinking differently leads to acting more productively. And so, when Hartley explained his idea about using stories to help those interested in considering the human side of trust administration, I was all for it.

When read and reread, these stories will stay in the reader's memory. Stories told by participants — beneficiaries, trustees, wealth advisors, attorneys and accountants — in their own voices are meant to promote new thinking and motivate action. Their informality spotlights the human and emotional side of trusts. Their innovations can lead you and yours out of the wilderness.

Our collection of positive narratives is presented as an alternative to the popular assumption that trust creation and trust administration must be tightly structured to avoid conflict and litigation. Hopefully the positive examples will provide a circuit-breaker to redirect the flow of negativity or "trust anxiety" that permeates the field.

When the trust process begins, or as challenges arise in administering and receiving trust proceeds, the goal is to create an effective new approach to the use of a trust. This new approach might start with a discussion that brings in all of the parties involved. Look for a process that would provide an opportunity for the trust-creator, trustee, professionals and beneficiary to get to know one other personally and regularly and for them all to know the family context in which the trust was created.

I believe that knowing one another as participants in the trust process is at the heart of what is positive about the 25 stories included in this book. Getting to deeply understand one another, and the relationships that provide the context for their life, maximizes the beneficiary/trustee relationship and the well-being of the family for generations. This takes perseverance, planning and resolve. It is the most significant first step and is the basis for continuing success.

MORE ABOUT MATURITY

Being a mature member of a family, a better-defined person, is a lifelong challenge but one that has benefit in work and friendship circles. It starts with appreciating how interconnected we all are, how infectious anxiety in a family can be, how our thinking and actions are profoundly affected by the relationships that surround us.

Maturity and self-definition mean four things to me, and for this chapter I relied on these four to enhance the beneficiary/trustee relationship. Evidence would be in the story entitled "The Unpopular Beneficiary" — the one where the trustee works to have the beneficiary assume responsibility for herself even when it made her uncomfortable.

1. The ability to know what you think and stand for;
2. The capacity to manage increasing levels of discomfort in important relationships;
3. The competence to live with differences between self and important others without trying to change the other; and
4. The aptitude to know what part you have been playing in relationships that are not working well.

SETTING THE STAGE

Chapters One and Two relied on the traditional mode of using the first part of the book to "introduce the authors." Now it's time to turn the microphone over to the storytellers — individuals who are trusted by the authors, yet can only be introduced to you as an anonymous group.

To keep this collection from feeling too random, each story comes with an opening and closing paragraph, crafted by the authors. Just enough to get you "oriented" each time, but not so much as to narrowcast the personalities or the content.

What else can be clarified regarding "process"? Eight points, none of them critical, but together they are meant to reassure the methodical reader that we've also been careful...

1. All but one story, the one that came to us in writing, has been put together from telephone interviews conducted from 2010 to 2012.

2. Each story is "verified" to the extent that at least one of us knows the storyteller and we endorse the authenticity of what he or she says.

3. Yet the stories are in no sense "case studies," because the storyteller is speaking from his or her own point of view, doing so naturally, not functioning as an academic or historian.

4. To preserve the sense of direct speech yet not convey a "raw" or jagged feel, we performed more than minor editing, including tweaking names and other identifying facts to preserve confidentiality. So please do not take the bulk of what you see in the stories as a "transcript."

5. Looser versions of some of these stories appeared on our website NavigatingTheTrustscape.com between July 2011 and September 2012. Newer stories, coming in after this book was completed, will take the place of those that launched this project on the web.

6. Following our edits, storytellers confirmed that their stories were told as they intended and that confidentiality was adequately protected.

7. But what if, in your opinion, a story just doesn't make sense? Go ahead and skip it! This is not a novel; each story has its own "plot," with many under 1,000 words; and therefore skipping one doesn't alter the intrinsic value of any other one.

8. Finally, when our own "spin" either resonates with you or strikes you as missing the point entirely, send us an email and say why using the address TrustWorthy@NavigatingTheTrustscape.com.

CHAPTER THREE: WHAT OTHERS DO

When they face a decision or course of action, Trustscapers typically wonder: "What do other families/beneficiaries/trustees do?"

Good question. And — given limited occasions to compare notes, privacy concerns, and (because of advisor professional codes) confidentiality — it's not easy finding answers.

What can you do? We humbly suggest that you make diligent use of this book. The half-dozen stories you are about to read offer windows — you will get to see and hear others tackle some of the concerns you might have:

- Parents speak with children about wealth and values.
- A beneficiary makes her trustees see her for who she is.
- A grandfather scours the country to find the right trustee.
- An aunt wrestles with making a gift that will "first do no harm."
- Beneficiaries help to restructure a family's trust.
- A look at the family tree prompts the telling of stories.

As you read the stories, notice that if you hold your head just right — and squint a bit — you just might see your reflection in the windows. Distorted, perhaps. Even so, some version of those reflections could be you.

PREPARE A NICE DINNER, BREAK OUT THE WINE

Family manifesto, family meeting, next generation's informed judgment — it's all here. And the storyteller — an experienced institutional trustee in the role of informal educator and counselor — shows that knowing how to present important information without taking sides can make all the difference.

As this story begins, I am the trust officer, and the grantors, husband and wife, are in their late forties. Theirs is first-generation wealth of about $100 million. They have three children — son 22, and two daughters, aged 19 and 17. The grantors are being very thoughtful about how to introduce their children to issues related to their family's wealth.

The husband calls one day and requests a review of the family manifesto. He sends me what must be 15 pages talking about his family's values, his views about America and free enterprise. I am quite taken by the manifesto's thoroughness and thoughtfulness.

It's also clear that he alone has written this. Rather than being a values statement produced "bottom-up" by the family, it's a "top-down" values statement. He is being paternal, saying *now hear this.*

I meet with him and his wife over breakfast to discuss the manifesto. He wants me to play devil's advocate, so I raise questions, starting with his assertion that children must have prenuptial agreements before marriage.

I contend that it is important to talk to children about prenuptial agreements before they announce that they are engaged. Insisting upon a prenuptial agreement after a child has announced that he or she is engaged will be interpreted in only one way: "My parents don't like my fiancée."

And so I inquire: "Are either of the children close to getting engaged?"

The question has touched a hot button. Husband and wife look at each other and she says, "Well, my son..." and he adds that "yeah, he..." Then comes this awkward silence punctuated by these half-completed thoughts. And finally the husband explains: "Well, our son has this long-term relationship..."

The son's relationship is with a girl from a family whose values are very different from those expressed in the manifesto. We talk a little bit about how to discuss this with the children and perhaps whittle the manifesto a bit to reflect what he would actually say to them.

They decide to have the conversation at their lake home — the most relaxing setting for the family and where they tend to have their best conversations. When the day comes, they prepare a lovely dinner; open a bottle of wine; sit down around the dining-room table — and introduce this subject. They speak about the importance of prenuptial agreements.

And then Dad and Mom put all the cards on the table. "Here's how much we're worth and here are the steps we're taking. We're assembling a team" — etc. To their surprise, their kids already know roughly how much the family is worth. And how did they find out? They had Googled their father and found holdings that were reported in 10-Ks.

The conversation goes surprisingly well. The kids know their father quite well and probably didn't expect this family meeting to be a democratic exercise. And they are fine with that.

After the family meeting, the son comes to me saying he wants to learn about prenuptials. Here is a chance to be his counselor. And so we do a tutorial.

Later on, their father says the neatest thing: "Our son needed to hear about prenuptial agreements for himself, and then make his own judgment." This is what you hope happens: The relationship is strong enough, and the counsel wise enough, that parents entrust their children with responsibilities and let them make informed judgments.

What are the themes to take from this story? One is a generational theme. These parents, today in their mid-fifties, approach their wealth and talk about their wealth very differently from how their own parents would have. And even though Dad remains very paternal, he is open to counsel and recognizes that if the children are going to grow and become mature wealth-owners themselves, they've got to play a role in the process.

And there are various ways to get at the values issue. One of them is the approach where Dad or Mom delivers the family manifesto. In this family, it has worked well to help shape estate-planning decisions. It also has helped to engage the kids in thoughtful management of their own.

A final theme: Family manifestos or mission statements aren't legally relevant to how we, as trustee, interpret trust instruments, except where some part of the manifesto or mission statement helps to reduce ambiguity in that trust agreement. In truth, when we have them — and we don't see them that often — we do read them for how they'll supplement our understanding of the family, its values, and the role that wealth is playing. They do inform our broader judgment.

From Dad's paternalistic manifesto to children's informed judgment in the span of a handful of years — I don't think the trust business gets any better than that.

Are you listening, Trustscapers? You've got everything to gain by putting together a declaration of your family's values. As this trustee says, "We do read them…"

I AM ME, NOT ONE OF EIGHT

Perhaps you will read this story and conclude that "slow and steady wins the race." Yet the subtler point is: It can't be a race. A different kind of meeting or conversation takes place, and then the process seems to stop. But — not really. The gains do arrive, in increments, even if the increments stretch themselves out.

A young woman was referred to me by one of the major banks. She was, and is, the eldest of eight children. She was sent to me because she and her brothers and sisters all were beneficiaries of quite substantial trusts that had been created for them by their grandparents. And the trusts were separate, so that each of them had their own funds.

There was a lot of addiction in the family and it played out in many of the members. I was assured, however, that she was not one of those in that condition. So I received her in the office and began to talk with her about what she wanted.

"Well," she explained, "what I'd like to do is to be seen by my trustees as an individual person, not one of eight children. Not only that, but I would like the trustees to listen to me each year about my interests and my goals for the trust, so they can help me with that." I replied: "If you'd like to do that, I would be happy to arrange a meeting with your trustees."

The trustees happened to be elderly men chosen by the grantors. They were, as you will soon see, very fixed in their views and their ways.

And so I continued: "Frankly, I'll need to know — before this meeting — what you've done over the years to individuate yourself and differentiate yourself not only from your brothers and sisters, but from everyone else in the world. Also, what have you done that would cause the trustees to acknowledge you as a separate person?"

Her reply: "Nothing."

"Well, that's okay — that's fine. I think we need to spend some time preparing you for this meeting." I explained, "I can assure you that the first meeting is not going to be a meeting in which you are going to achieve any of your goals."

Very disappointed, she asked why the first meeting might feel pointless.

"Because these men are likely to have a view of you as one of eight troubled people. They are simply not likely to accept, after a single meeting, that you are not only different from those people, but that they should treat you differently than how they treat those people."

"Yes," she said, "that makes sense to me."

We had two or three coaching sessions in my office, and then set up a meeting with the trustees. We invited the banker who was servicing my client and the trust accounts to come with us.

We arrived at the office of these gentlemen who, as I said, were quite elderly. The wonderful young woman presented herself. She asked the trustees at the beginning of the meeting, "Will you receive me as myself? Will you listen to me as myself? Will you suspend your likely thought that I am simply one of eight to be treated the same way?"

After nice pleasantries, of course they said they would. And we all know they couldn't. It would be impossible.

It was very clear to me after the first few questions they asked, and after she made a lovely presentation about herself, that they had their minds made up. They saw their role as basically babysitting eight lucky sperm-club kids, all of whom were dependent people and many of them seriously addicted.

By the end of the meeting, however, they began to look strangely at us. We had created a problem for them.

We said, "Thank you very much," and we left.

My client was very anxious to have another meeting right away.

"No," I said, "we need to let six months go by. Then I want you to come back. I want to coach you some more. I want you to tell the trustees again all the things you told them before, because I promise they won't remember everything you said. I also want you to tell them what you would like to do with your life."

Back we went, six months later, to see those elderly gentlemen. This time I spoke to the banker before the meeting, because I sensed that he was an advocate for my client. What a delight to discover that he had wanted to be her advocate, but until then hadn't known how to treat her individually and differently from her brothers and sisters. Why? Because he himself had not had any experience in doing that.

I can still see the trustees all sitting around the table at one end, and us sitting at the other end. My client made her presentation as she had before. Then she said, "I'd like to tell you what my dreams are, how this trust can enhance my life."

These old gentlemen started to have wide eyes as she expressed not only who she was, but also the dream that she had — to become a sculptor, a serious sculptor — along with marrying and having a full life, and physically moving away from the family.

At the end of the meeting, the senior trustee, or so he expressed himself to be, said, "I am troubled." And then, and then only, did I know that she had made an impact.

Some would say that "troubled" is a strange word after all this work. "No," I thought, "if a trustee is troubled, it means that he has a problem that he didn't expect to have. His normal means of responding will not apply, and he is going to have to do some hard work." That's why it was a sign of impending progress to hear: "I am troubled."

"Yes," I replied to the trustee, "I imagine you *are* troubled." And then I empathized with him for about 10 minutes. The young woman sat there spellbound.

Up until then, I had been carefully quiet as I could be. Now I became, in a sense, her advocate, expressing to the trustee how powerful I thought her dream was; how lucky I thought he and his co-trustees were that one of these eight was going to have a good life; and they could be the means by which that good life, in part, could be achieved.

And so we left. Once again, we did not ask for any money.

About two months later, I got a call from the senior trustee. He said to me: "We have been sitting here stewing over your client and your presentation. And, while we would really prefer to treat all eight people the same exact way, we now realize that we can't. This young woman has gotten under our skins. Would you arrange for her to come back with you and the banker? Let's talk about what we might be able to do."

So we did. The end of the story is that that this young woman did relocate and has become a very important sculptor in the area of the country where she lives. She married a wonderful man, and they have a great marriage. And the trustees provided her with much of the means to fulfill her dream.

The moral of the story? Had she not decided that she would courageously individuate and differentiate — if she had not done the hard work of establishing who she was in a world of illusion about who she was — then nothing would have happened. But she stepped forward with courage, perseverance, and patience. Over time, the trustees were prepared to make a change in their own view of the world because a responsible and mature human being came and asked them to do so.

If a beneficiary sits home waiting for the trustee to change, nothing is going to happen. The beneficiary must be ready to say: "I am prepared for a journey with my trustees to educate them about who I am and about my goals and aspirations, so they, in turn, can come on that journey with me."

And it is by the beneficiary that the first steps must be taken.

Very true. You'll note that our storyteller started with the magic question — what have you done that would cause the trustees to acknowledge you as a separate person? — and kept it in focus. His client had an answer, and also came to understand that it would take time for their audience to hear it.

MY GRANDFATHER'S GIFT

This story is a tribute — indeed, a salute — from a beneficiary to his lifelong trustee. It is among the most positive of all the positive examples offered in this book. And don't miss how a trustee slipped into the role of mentor, even at a relatively young age.

The trust of which I am the beneficiary was created by my grandfather, who passed away when I was only nine years old. He and I were very close, particularly during the final year of his life. Due to my young age, he and I never directly discussed wealth, trusts, or financial planning.

He did, however, through his actions, begin laying a solid foundation for responsible decision-making.

In one of my earliest memories of him, he demonstrated honesty and integrity. I was about six years old or so and my mother and I were visiting him in New York City. It was around six in the evening. I was playing on the floor with some toy or another and starting to get thoroughly bored. My mother and grandfather were having "an adult conversation" that did not interest me in the least.

"Grandpa, when can we go to dinner?" I asked. "In five minutes," he replied.

Every young child has heard such words and knows they mean at some as yet undetermined time — and probably a long time from right now. But I watched the clock and, after five minutes, announced: "It has been five minutes."

"Then it is time for us to go to dinner," my grandfather said, rising from his chair and grabbing his jacket.

That level of honesty and integrity would stick with me.

Throughout my childhood, my grandfather never gave me a toy. Instead, he gave me books — one at a time. The day a book was finished, he would take me to the bookstore to get another one.

He also paid for all of my education, including activities such as ski school. From these examples, I learned valuable lessons. For example, to be somewhat frugal with money.

The most wonderful aspect of having wealth is not the toys it will buy, but rather the opportunities it provides. While "toys" like Porsches and Rolexes might be nice, it is far more important to be able to work in a career that one enjoys and to live where one wants.

Despite my grandfather having passed away when I was rather young, I did learn some of his thoughts about wealth and money-management through my mother. Fortunately, he was willing to share his thoughts and philosophies regarding investment and financial planning with her. She has continued this open dialog thus allowing his voice and thoughts to reach me through her.

The way my trusts were structured allowed me to learn about wealth, investment and financial planning in steps. Two trusts were created for me. A smaller trust dissolved when I turned 21. I had the right to dissolve the larger one at the age of 35.

I have been very fortunate to have a great relationship with the two co-trustees who oversee my trusts. One is my mother. The other is a man who was selected by my Eastern European-born, Jewish grandfather. At the time my grandfather selected him, this man was young and a recent law-school graduate. What could have attracted an old Jewish man to a young Mormon attorney? I believe it was three things: One, they were both very intelligent; two, they both had a very strong sense of the importance of family; and finally, they both were extremely ethical men.

Joseph (the young Mormon attorney) has been a part of my life since I was about eight years old. He would visit the house frequently to meet with my mother about various family matters. Even when I was a young child, he did things to reach out to me.

The first pocket calculator (assuming you had very large pockets) I ever saw was one that Joseph had with him. He took the time to show it to me and to let me play with it (in 1974, this thing was really cool).

Several years later, knowing that I was very into skiing and the Olympics, he brought me a huge pin on button that said "Park City's Great Olympic Hope." These events might sound trivial, but they started to establish a friendship between a child (me) and an adult (Joseph). Joseph went on to become my mentor in financial and legal matters as well as serving as trustee for the trust established for me.

My education in financial responsibility started at an early age. Rarely was I just given toys. I had to put what I wanted on a gift list and wait for a special occasion like a birthday or holiday. Otherwise, I had to save my allowance. I started working at the age of 15 in order to have spending money of my own. This helped to teach me the value of money and to learn how to manage what money I had.

I was told about the trusts that had been established for me at about the age of 16 or so. I was invited to all meetings with the stockbrokers, bond managers and attorneys in order to start learning about asset management. I was informed about all of the decisions being made and the logic behind the decisions.

This five-year "apprenticeship" combined with discussions with my mother about her and my grandfather's investment principles left me fairly well prepared to take over management of my smaller trust at age 21. It was both exciting and intimidating to me at that age to come into what seemed like a very large amount of money.

It was initially tempting to run out and buy lots of exciting expensive "toys." A small bit of discretion, however, says that if you do that in very short order you will use up all of the money. One of the lessons that had been passed to me from my grandfather through my mother was not to spend principal. Leave the principal alone and only use profit for consumption (preferably not all of the profits). By virtue of following this advice and generally listening to the financial advisors that had been managing this smaller trust until I turned 21, that account has continued to grow quite nicely over the past twenty-some odd years.

Being the beneficiary of a trust may feel a bit like having won the lottery or, on the opposite end, could feel like someone (the trustee) is blocking you from gaining access to what is rightfully yours. I would like to suggest that neither attitude is a good one to adopt. I think that I can offer some insight into how to avoid these two extremes.

Initially, it helps if the beneficiary understands why the trust was established in the first place. I came to this understanding gradually over many years of open discussions with my mother and Joseph. The smaller "age 21" trust was set up largely to teach me about financial planning and asset management. I believe that it was also set up to allow my mother a chance to determine just how responsible I would be with a larger amount of money.

The larger trust, which I had the right to dissolve at age 35, contained substantially more money and was a bit more complex from a management standpoint. This trust was invested in not only stocks, but also bonds and oil properties. While I am still not an expert in any of these fields, the additional years from age 21 to age 35 allowed me to get familiar with these different types of investments.

Over the years, I also came to realize that one of the tremendous benefits of having this larger sum of money in a trust is that it protects it from creditors. This protection combined with an excellent relationship with the trustees led me to choose not to dissolve this trust at age 35. I have come to realize that, properly managed, this money will continue to grow and be available to take care of my family for many generations. The protection of those assets has thus become a priority.

The situation where the beneficiary winds up feeling like the trust is an obstacle never really happened to me. Most of the credit for this goes to my grandfather and Joseph. The way that they crafted the trust and the guidelines that spell out what sort of expenditures the trustee can cover were well thought-out and fairly thorough.

The crafting of a good set of guidelines is a bit like the framing of the U.S. Constitution. The guidelines should be detailed enough to cover all of the needs that the trust-grantor had in mind, but also flexible enough to be interpreted by the trustee to cover future occurrences that the grantor may not have been able to envision. Because the future is dynamic and none of us has a crystal ball, it is important that the trustee be able to use their best judgment to interpret the intentions of the grantor.

As for the beneficiary, it is equally important to become familiar with the guidelines of the trust. This helps to prevent potential problems between the beneficiary and the trustee. The relationship will be much smoother if the beneficiary is not making unreasonable requests of the trustee. An unreasonable request would be one that the guidelines of the trust obviously prevent the trustee from being able to accommodate.

The guidelines of my trust spell out that it can be used for my "health, education, and well-being." Although the first two items seem fairly cut and dried, they could be open to some interpretation. For example, "health" could strictly be interpreted to mean visits to a medical doctor — but what if I as the beneficiary wanted to go see an acupuncturist? Would a dietitian fall into the realm of "health"? How about a personal trainer?

"Education" could be strictly interpreted to mean primary school, high school and college at accredited institutions. Would the costs of studying abroad fall into the realm of "education"? Pushing it just a bit further, a course on how to paint classic nudes? These would all be questions the trustee would have to answer while talking into account the grantor's intentions. I imagine that Joseph's longstanding relationship with my family has helped him to interpret what my grandfather's intentions might have been.

The final category of "well-being" is even more open to interpretation than the first two. In general, it has covered things like the purchase of a house (having shelter) and the purchase of a car (to be able to get to work).

Having been the beneficiary of this trust for quite a while now, I have become fairly familiar with what things the trust can pay for, since many expenses tend to reoccur on a regular basis. That is not to say that I do not periodically come up with something new.

My first step is to look at my request and see if I think it falls within the guidelines of the trust and how those guidelines have been interpreted over the years. If I decide that my request will meet the trust's requirements for disbursement to me, I try to come up with a well-reasoned "argument" for why I feel that my request is reasonable (the reason can never be "because I want it"). Then, when I contact the trustees, I am in a position to help explain to them how my request works within the guidelines of the trust.

When I am not sure if something is going to fall within the guidelines of the trust, my first step is to ask. Sometimes I have been surprised to hear Joseph's answer: "Yes the trust guidelines allow for a disbursement for that."

A prime example was the purchase of sport fishing boat. The trust purchased the boat and keeps it within the trust. The trust allows my family and me to use the boat. I in turn pay for fuel and routine maintenance. Because the boat is kept properly maintained, it's my hope that, if the trust sells the boat at some future date, it will be able to do so for the same amount as the original purchase price.

I try to remember that if I am careful about how much I consume of the trust's profits, there will be sufficient assets to take care of my family for many generations to come. The final piece of the puzzle has to be the things that the trustee does to create and maintain a good working relationship with the beneficiary. I have already touched on a few of these qualities.

In my case, it certainly helped that I had a very high opinion of my grandfather and, almost by default, the people that he chose to put into positions of responsibility. His faith in Joseph helped to "stack the deck" in Joseph's favor, but that was merely the beginning of a very long road (in truth one of the longest-lasting relationships that I have ever had with another person). The little things that Joseph did as an adult to reach out to me as a child were critical in the development of a rapport between the two of us.

Did you notice the symmetry? This thoughtfully chosen trustee exemplifies the same values of integrity, love of family, and wealth as opportunity that the trust-creator did.

TIPTON REDUX? A GREAT GIFT, WITH MENTORS

This story commences with a very high level of awareness and integrity. It especially shows the innovative power of spreading the mentoring function among a group of people.

A remarkable woman wanted to discuss something that had been burdening her for some time: She wanted to make significant financial gifts to nieces and nephews, but was reluctant to act for fear she would do harm.

She had studied very carefully the question of how money integrates well — or poorly — into a human life. She knew that gifts often create sadness and trouble. So she asked me to help her construct a plan to make the gifts in such a way that would, to the best of our belief, avoid doing harm. We both agreed that the answer to the question of whether we could help these nieces and nephews was something that she could not know. But we could start out with the principle of doing no harm.

Because substantial financial resources coming to these young people looked very grim in terms of doing harm, we felt that a direct gift could not be successful. They came from a very broken home with a lot of addictions and very little money. Some of them had had addiction problems of their own. They had some education — not great educations, but some education.

Thus, we decided to create trusts. We thought that each niece and nephew should have his or her own trust, as this would be a better way for us to find out if we could help their dreams come true.

The important question then became: "What role could the trustee play?" Was it enough to find an enlightened trustee who would understand the risk of causing harm here? One willing to seek to ameliorate the condition of each of these young people and have this money integrate into their lives successfully?

We found a pretty good trustee. We all agreed, including the trustee, that additional guidance was needed. So we created a mentoring committee to help the trustee integrate the funds as successfully as possible into the lives of these young people. We solicited for that role people we felt would be not only interested in the well-being of these young people, but who also would be open to learning a great deal about themselves and about the role of a fiduciary at its highest calling — the enhancement of another person's life. We found those people.

Now comes *The Millionaire* television drama. In the 1950s, there was a great program in which, each week on television, a gift of one million dollars would be made to a person completely out of the blue. The gentleman who wrote the check was named John Beresford Tipton.

A meeting was called for the young family members and their parent, the mentors (I was a mentor), and the institutional trustee. Only one of us had ever met these young people. As a group, we were going to tell them about their aunt's gift and her dreams for them — not that different from *The Millionaire* series.

We arrived. The young people had no idea why we, or they, were there. Their parent, who did know what was going to happen, had kept mum about it. We told these young people of their remarkable good fortune not only, frankly, as a matter of good fortune, but also with a message about the dangers of financial wealth suddenly introduced into a human's life.

Now I think you can imagine that, as we were talking to these young people, all they could hear was their good fortune. They could not have heard anything else we said, and they didn't. Nor do I think that anyone else would have been able to.

We did talk to them about what the nature of a trust was, which they seemed able to absorb at some level. We said to them: "Now, let's go home. In a couple of months, we are going to come back and meet with each of you and see if we can begin a journey together. A journey to the successful integration of your aunt's gift into your life, so that it enhances your life rather than making you a dependent, unfree person."

For many years, we were on that journey together. I'm retired now and others have succeeded me. What I can say is that the lives of the nieces and nephews have clearly been enhanced. For a while, even with the best of intentions, there were moments of profligacy and poor choices. However, after 10 years of the journey, I'm very happy to say that all of the young people now are flourishing.

Now, does that mean that they are incredibly enlightened, awakened people? No. They are themselves. But the most important thing about being themselves is that they are achieving the level of freedom that they are capable of achieving, which is every human being's journey, I believe. And the gift of the aunt is helping that journey.

What was needed beyond the gift, however, was a team — a persevering trustee backed by persevering mentors who never for a moment doubted that these gifts could be a great experience for these people. We stood on a high ground and occasionally, when people got a little wobbly, leaned down and gently stood them up again and said: "Come on, we can solve this together."

The mentors also made mistakes. We didn't get it right every time. But we all agree — the young people, the mentors and the trustee — that this was a grand experiment: Could their aunt's gift not only do them no harm but also enhance their lives and bring their dreams to life?

The greatness of this story, interestingly, is the story of the founder's awareness of the potential consequences of *The Millionaire*'s gift.

It is important to realize that the donor's intent is so critical to the outcome. Failure to understand the motivation for a gift so often leads to a failed playing forward of that action.

And so I would end like this: These trusts are gifts, they are not transfers. The founder had a deep, deep desire that she make gifts in the highest sense.

Every beneficiary should be so lucky — so blessed — to begin such an experiment with a loving and wise family elder setting the parameters; and a committed group of mentors supporting the beneficiaries as well as the trustee. In some ways, you just heard a tale of "greatness." It supports the importance of thinking carefully about even the positive events in life.

"I WONDER IF WE CAN..."

Among other things, our storyteller shows the power of being able to reply to general questions — not with answers (either general or specific), but with other questions, questions that are wide-ranging and thought-provoking all at the same time. Try this in a family setting, and watch the barriers fall.

The original trust had been created in the 1980s purely as a tax play. The grantor seeded it with about $400,000 of value that he fully expected to grow. And grow impressively it did.

From a strictly quantitative analysis, it was a wonderful play. The problem was that the grantor, at that point in his life, was all about tax-efficiency. As time went on — his children came of age, got married, he had his first grandchild — he did more planning.

This man read Jay Hughes' book *Family Wealth*[1], and asked him to come speak to his family. What came out of all this was a severe case of grantor's remorse. He concluded that he had set up his trust for failure. How so? Because the purpose had been to hog as much money out of the tax system as possible, as far into the future as possible — and then, in effect, dump it all on family members.

He asked me, "What can we do about this?" We went through all kinds of machinations until it was clear that the only thing to do was a reformation[2] of the trust.

The grantor asked his adult children and their spouses to drive the reformation. He thought this would be a real learning exercise for them because passing down this level of wealth would have considerable effect on them, and their descendants as well.

Reformation of the trust required that all of the beneficiaries be represented and work together. The grantor's children, their spouses, and a court-appointed *guardian ad litem* (to represent the interests of unborn beneficiaries) met with the trustee and advisors, including me, over the course of several years. Some combination of the beneficiaries and advisors had conversations about once a month. And the whole family met together three times a year.

One of the things that I found interesting was that the grantor's children had come from an environment where their parents had — to a startling degree — relieved them of responsibility for thinking. "The trust will take care of that. Don't worry about it," was the belief.

So here was the first time that they were not only able to have a voice, but able to start to look for one.

As we discussed the reformation, they often asked me, "What do other people do?" And I said, "Other people do what's right for them. What we need to do is what's right for you. So, I'm not going to tell you."

---

[1] Hughes, James E., Jr., *Family Wealth — Keeping it in the Family*, Bloomberg Press (2004).
[2] Redo the trust with the court's approval.

Instead I asked them to consider questions such as:

"What is it you want your children to experience in life even if you're not here to help them experience it?"

"What is it that you would like the financial assets to mean to your children, your grandchildren and beyond?"

"What do you want your legacy to be?" And here "legacy" means: "What will your beneficiaries think, feel and say when they hear your name?"

They became really thoughtful in their new role as trust-designers rather than just as beneficiaries. It was an absolutely amazing experience to watch the grantor's children and their spouses grow and learn.

The original trust contained pretty standard distribution language. The trustee, at his discretion, was permitted to make distributions to beneficiaries for health, education, maintenance and support. The beneficiaries wanted to make this trust more purposeful.

I asked them: "What is it that you want? Forget about the old document. You can define 'education' broadly or narrowly. What feels right to you?"

The conversations started shifting. The participants were drilling down.

"All right, one of our beneficiaries — one of our children or grandchildren — says, 'I want to go to Florence and study art for six months.' Does that feel like education to you?"

It was interesting to watch the ebb and flow of these kinds of questions. "Well, he'll just be a bum in Italy."

"Really? What if he spent the last three years studying art and he wants to be an art history professor? Wouldn't that be worthwhile?"

"Yeah."

"In other words, as long as he's qualified to have the experience, then it's a good experience."

"Yeah, that's exactly right."

They started responding less knee-jerk and were now thinking more broadly and meaningfully. They did the same thing for the other standards. "What does 'health' mean? Maintenance? Support?"

One of the principles developed from these conversations was a kind of family safety net. Everybody will have food, everybody will have shelter, everybody will have health care.

They started to understand that trusts could achieve certain results without handing cash over to somebody. It was eye-opening for them to see the big difference between expressly deciding what could be, as opposed to accepting the boilerplate "what everyone else does."

I encouraged the beneficiaries to start with the question, "I wonder if we can…" based on a goal they wanted to accomplish. They came back with questions such as these:

"I wonder if we can have some way where we can each be independent of each other — so we don't feel like we are tripping over each other's business — but at the same time retain the power of community and the ability to work together as a family?"

They came up with an incredibly interesting solution on their own. Each beneficiary's family would have a separate share of the trust — funded up to a certain dollar level — with the rest in a "pot" for the family as a whole.

"We think we know best about our children and our grandchildren. I wonder if we could have some parental input into the decisions that the trustee makes for our children?"

They decided to establish a board of family advisors within the trust document itself. The board will give non-binding input to the trustee prior to any distribution being made.

Families I work with reach a point where they are able to work together like this. They often don't realize how much work they did to get to that point — understanding their roles, understanding how they interact, understanding that wealth is a continuum. Having flexibility to design a path through their different opinions.

Now the grantor's children are doing their own planning. They are mentally prepared to deal with this responsibility. It's not a foreign idea for them to be thinking about, "Well, what do we want to accomplish for our children?"

Perhaps the family process was as eye-opening for you as it was for the people taking part in it! And don't neglect this other point, which the story's opening only hinted at: When a trust is designed solely for tax-efficiency, the long-term result can be "hogging money from the government." But that takes place at the cost of keeping growth and responsibility from a rising generation.

IT WAS THE DAY BEFORE CHRISTMAS

Most lawyers aren't trained to initiate the sort of conversations that illuminate family themes and values. Neither are money-managers. Which leads to an opportunity for the trustee, as well as for certain family members. This next story showcases the power of the "qualitative" as much as any in our collection.

I am trust officer for the family of a fellow who is selling a business on the west coast for a lot of money (in the range of $100-150 million). He recognizes that this is a very important event for his family and seeks broader counsel: What does it mean for his family to go from owning a closely held business to owning liquid assets?

He convenes a family meeting and invites me to attend. I agree — notwithstanding the fact that the meeting is going to take place on the day before Christmas (which is the only time that will work for the various family members). Charlie Collier, Harvard's Senior Philanthropic Advisor at this time, is invited as well.

We fly out on the prior evening. The patriarch, matriarch, six adult children and their spouses, Charlie and I meet at the family's vacation home in the mountains. We enjoy a long dinner and have a lovely time. The next day is reserved for the serious topics.

On the morning of the 24th, with the breakfast dishes cleared, we're sitting around their large dining-room table. Charlie turns to the patriarch and says: "Jack, tell me about your grandparents." Jack starts with the usual things — where they were born, where they grew up, and so on. My role is to draw the family tree and write down themes. After about 15 minutes of listening to Jack speak, everyone is rapt.

So Jack is telling stories as Charlie guides him through the family tree. We get about 90 minutes into this — working down from his grandparents' generation — and this family is transfixed. Now we're hearing about Jack's generation. We get to a story about his sister, who had a very difficult life. Jack's telling a story about her and — in the midst of telling how she had overcome some very difficult challenges — he breaks down in tears.

Charlie very graciously says: "You know, I just realized we've been at this for an hour and a half — and this is a very good time for a break. We can reconvene in about 15 minutes."

I leave the room so the family can be by themselves. The matriarch follows me out into the hall. Tears are streaming down her cheeks. She grabs both my hands — just grasps them firmly — and she looks me straight in the eye and says: "I have never heard these stories." Then she says something even more powerful: "I've never even seen this side of him."

And you realize that you've been a participant in something really extraordinary. With Charlie's skilled guidance, this family has unearthed some exceptional experiences that are going to inform their lives — the way they manage money, the way they plan estates. Really extraordinary.

It was a turning point for me, seeing how this kind of inquiry in the hands of someone as gifted as Charlie can make remarkable things happen. It was probably the most powerful experience of my professional career.

As part of laying a foundation for understanding the impact of financial wealth, we now regularly invite clients to talk about the values that shaped their families. Lawyers aren't trained to have these kinds of conversations — which is okay, because this is a responsibility that belongs with the trustee.

Our storytelling trustee witnessed the value of describing the context in which the family's wealth was created. And we can see why the "family tree" — when not accompanied by details in stories and conversations — is not much more than lines and dates on a diagram. It's a very good starting point, no doubt. But keep going, ask questions, and especially allow space for thoughtful and complete conversations.

CHAPTER FOUR:
DILEMMAS TRANSCENDED

Don't overlook the value of trusts when it comes to transcending family dilemmas. One thoughtful member of a trustscape system can make a positive difference for the entire system and its members. You are about to meet trust-creators, trustees, beneficiaries and advisors faced with vexing situations.

THE SEVEN-YEAR STRUGGLE

We always hear that any plan is better than no plan. In this case, the trust's plan was mechanical: One-third at age 25, one-third at 30, and one-third at 35. When a legal judgment intervened, that sequence was put at risk. What was left? A trustee keeping his thinking open as to the capacity of, and possible futures for, the beneficiary; and a beneficiary showing a readiness to take up the challenges. Both have an appreciation for the long horizon ahead.

A young man — we'll call him Hank — went out drinking with his college buddies one evening. He ended up in a serious altercation outside of the club. Hank was barely bruised in the fight, but the two people he attacked with a broken bottle suffered serious injuries. They sued Hank.

Orphaned years before, Hank was the beneficiary of a trust that provided periodic income distributions and would pay out principal in staged distributions based on his age. The first major principal distribution, one-third of the trust, would occur on Hank's 25th birthday. By age 35, the entire trust would be distributed to him.

I was trustee of Hank's trust.

Prior to the accident, Hank and I had met twice in person — once as he turned 18 years old, and another time during his summer break from college. My other conversations with him had been by phone and email. In fact, I learned of the brawl through an email requesting help to find an attorney, and to provide funds for the legal proceeding.

A few months later, we met face-to-face. This was our first meaningful meeting. It took place a week before Hank's deposition.

I suggested we leave the formality of the office and find a quiet restaurant. Once there, I asked Hank to help me understand what had happened at the bar. The request was made with a sincere intention to hear, and to do so without judgment. As I listened, I felt Hank's deep remorse over the harm he had inflicted.

I also picked up the anxiety and fear he was feeling about the legal process. We talked through the different outcomes his attorney had warned him about. If the court awarded the injured men a sum of money, because alcohol had been involved, the bankruptcy laws in Hank's state would not release him from the debt. It appeared quite possible that Hank was going to lose a lot.

He asked me to predict the outcome; how bad would the judgment be, and would it hang over his head for the rest of his lifetime? I agreed to speak with his defense attorney, seek counsel from a bankruptcy lawyer, and look for creative suggestions. He wanted to have it settled as quickly as possible and avoid the stress of the upcoming deposition.

I wasn't able to "make this all go away" as Hank had hoped. He had to go through the deposition. But an offer was crafted and his defense attorney presented it to the attorneys representing the two injured young men. We negotiated a settlement where the trust would make an initial lump sum payment to each young man and then monthly distributions for seven years.

Hank was told that, during these seven years, he would not be receiving income distributions from the trust. He also heard that — if he wanted to preserve his trust principal so there would be something for him down the road — he would have to get a job to support himself.

Hank agreed to this alternative, which would preserve a significant portion of his trust.

He seemed to grasp, on some level, that our work together had gone much beyond the usual relationship between a trustee and beneficiary. I had listened to him, offered positive suggestions, and stepped into a role as advocate and translator to help him understand the legal process.

During the seven years, Hank's journey proved difficult. But he began to understand that I'd be there for him — not just as the manager of the trust assets, not just as the person who had the power to make principal distributions to him, and not just as the person who made sure we were in compliance with federal or state tax filings — but also to support his growing maturity.

We talked at least once a year. During our conversations I provided positive reinforcement as I saw him holding down a job, pursuing his degree, and living frugally.

This helped to diminish the formality of the trustee role in Hank's mind and paint it with more of a "mentoring" brush. I did not say, "It's my way or no way." Rather, suggestions put forth were an invitation as opposed to a direction to do this, that, and the other thing. Our relationship blossomed.

After that seven-year struggle, Hank called. He had gotten married and wanted to sit down and plan for his future. Hank's questions burned brightly. How might his trust accelerate the attainment of his dreams and hopes?

I flew to where he and his wife were living. Over the course of a three-hour conversation, we talked about their goals, hopes, dreams for the future and how the trust might support them in that. We talked about the ways in which he was taking accountability for the things he had messed up previously.

Losing the income stream he'd been taking for granted before the accident had been a wake-up call. He hadn't really been living his life the way he wanted. Now, with the encouragement he was receiving from his wife, he was making better decisions.

A few years later, I met with Hank and his wife again. They were feeling the strains of a growing young family in terms of money and escalating responsibilities. They were expecting their first child. Their minds were on the type of support they could count on from his trust — issues such as whether his wife would be able to stay home rather than keep working full-time.

The birth of his son transformed Hank. Instead of being focused only on the present, he began to worry about things like paying for college.

A conversation with Hank and his wife deepened our professional relationship. I suggested that, at Christmas time every year, he and his wife write a letter to their infant son describing all of the things he'd done the previous year that made them proud or filled them with a sense of awe.

The conclusion to the story occurred a few years after the injury settlement agreement was fully satisfied. Hank was approaching his 35th birthday. The balance of the trust would be distributed to him. We talked about what that meant and how he wanted to receive the assets.

Over the course of that conversation, Hank paused to reflect with gratitude on the Christmas letter suggestion from years earlier. He said that they now had two sons and were writing letters to each of them. He related how wonderful that practice had become — how he and his wife read the letters to their sons at Christmas and the joy it brought to their family. They were keeping the letters in binders to give to their sons as each emerges into adulthood.

Hank thanked me profusely. It wasn't thanks for the "job well done" managing the trust assets. Nor for helping settle the lawsuit. Rather, the gratitude was for helping him mature, as father and husband, and for how good he felt about the legacy that he was leaving his sons through the Christmas letters.

For trustees who are reading this story, the one insight I hope you will take away from my experience with Hank is: Don't underestimate the ability of beneficiaries to recover from their own foibles and mistakes. Don't make the mistake of painting them with colors that reflect where they were when you first met them. Instead, be open to the possibility that, just as you and I change, they can change, too — morphing into something quite different from what you saw at an earlier age.

And, for the beneficiaries who read this, I hope this story gives you a glimpse of how your trustee might support your journey beyond just signing distribution checks. Be willing to show him or her that your door is open to a deeper connection and a "thinking partnership."

A trustee listening with full attention, suspending the tendency to judge, and willing to help navigate dangerous passages, and a beneficiary taking the initiative and making the sacrifices "preserved a significant portion of his trust." More importantly, in this case the trust served its purpose: It supported, rather than impaired, the beneficiary's higher functioning.

THE ROCKY ROAD TO FREEDOM

The storyteller "didn't grow up with any discipline as it relates to money," and her occasional attempts to achieve financial literacy had gone nowhere. Then one day, with a nudge from Dad and a trustee with "just the right mix of being firm and being kind," the road to freedom begins.

I grew up in a family of my father, mother, brother and sister. I'm the oldest of the three siblings.

My dad and his brothers grew up on a farm. They had very little. Their family was poor. My grandfather died when my father was seven. My grandmother was a schoolteacher. She raised eight kids.

Dad and his brothers started a company that, after becoming publicly traded, reached a ranking of #27 on the Fortune 100.

Once my father and his brothers had all of their success in business, my father's priority was to give my brother, sister and me the kind of freedom that he had never had. Having needed to work from a very young age, he discouraged me from working (and I need to emphasize that he didn't mean any harm by that). He also gave us a lot of freedom, which was great.

Dad knew what kind of world he wanted for us. Yet my parents never told us much about money or educated us in what is now known as "financial literacy." Mostly my dad just gave me money when I needed it or asked for it. The point is, I didn't grow up with any discipline as it relates to money and planning, or anything like that.

My dad would sometimes say I was spending too much money and should spend less. The problem was that no numbers were attached to his statement. It was all too vague for me. I would try to remember to spend less, and did so for a little while. But that didn't lead to any type of quantitative changes.

In those days, I was very involved in the world of horses — even then, a pretty expensive endeavor. I guess you'd say that's what created what my father felt were a lot of expenses. He'd keep asking, "Would you spend less?" or say with firmness: "I want you to spend less." However he would convey that message, I really wouldn't go along.

I used to go see him in his office a lot because I liked seeing him there. He had this great secretary that I adored. One day I went in and, before he barely had said hello, he stood up, grabbed his hat, and said, "We are walking up to the bank." His energy was a clue that something was up — but I had no idea what.

When we got to the bank, he introduced me to a banker named Bill. My father said, "What is going to happen here is you and I are no longer going to communicate about money. When you need money or however you and Bill want to set it up, you are going to deal with him and not with me."

I thought: "Well, that is kind of weird." But my father was quite serious about it. Why this change? He said it was because he had asked me to spend less money and I had not done so. I hadn't taken the request very seriously.

My dad had never been very good at saying no to me. Many fathers are like this with their daughters. He finally realized that he needed to step out of the picture. So he said: "Bill is going to work out a budget with you, and you'll be working with him on all of this from here on." He explained that a trust he had for me had been moved to the bank, and this was the money that Bill would use to give to me when I needed it.

That was really my first exposure to the whole concept of a trust. Looking back, I would say that this introduction, and new relationship with Bill, had the potential to be terrible. Fortunately, I adored my father. Though thinking the new set-up weird, I wanted to cooperate.

For a long time, I had wanted to become more financially literate. I had made some attempts, but they were very poor attempts. I had enrolled in a class in economics, which was a disaster. Because I didn't have any preparation for it (my Masters is in English) I was in over my head from Day One. I don't even know why I picked economics other than it had to do with numbers. The class was really hard. I stuck it out but it was horrible, and very discouraging.

Another time, I asked my father if I could talk with our accountant in order to try to understand taxes and anything financial. My dad said, "Yes." When I went to see our accountant, he started talking way over my head. I wasn't savvy enough to realize that some people who are great at what they do are horrible teachers. That was the case with this man. Once again, I felt intimidated.

Here's one more. I met a man at church. He was some kind of financial professional. I asked him if he would teach me about investments and he said he would. I went to his office to meet with him and it quickly became evident that all he wanted from me was an introduction to my father. I felt really hurt by that.

There are so many kinds of wrong turns you can make when you are young. I didn't have the right teachers, I didn't know where to look, and I didn't know the right questions to ask. Though trying to "grow up" financially, I had failed again and again. Maybe this had influenced my father to change the set-up totally — he probably knew most of the things that I had tried to do.

When introduced to Bill, I was 30 years old. I saw this new relationship as possibly a time when I could learn. Despite the surprise, I wasn't entirely against what Dad said was the new set-up. Bill was pretty nice, so I didn't have any bad feelings about him. I trusted my father completely, and figured he knew what he was doing.

The first meeting with Bill was kind of, "Hello, how are you?" Bill told me to come back in a few days and we would get started.

At our next meeting, the first thing he asked me was: "How much do you spend every month?" I had no idea — absolutely no idea. I was embarrassed because I figured most people were able to answer that question. So I told him, "I really don't have any idea."

He said, "We are going to need to know that, because it's basic. For the coming months, I will make sure there is money in the checking account. About how much will you need?" I guessed an amount.

During that first month, I had to keep track of what was actually being spent. I did so and took the information back to him. Based on that, we created a budget, which we projected for the year. I thought this would be okay.

So now I was living on a budget. Of course, before long, by about the 25th of the month, I had run completely out of money. I called Bill. "I'm so sorry but I ran out of money and I need you to put more money in my checking account."

"Sorry," Bill replied, "but you know that isn't the way this works. You are a smart young woman. I am sure you can figure out how to handle the situation."

"No, seriously — I need you to put some money in my account."

"We made a budget based on your spending and you've got a week to go until the first of next month. I know you can figure this out."

That was it — the end of the conversation. He hung up. He wouldn't budge. And I remember hanging up the phone and thinking, "Wow, I don't have any money." I looked around the cupboards and thought about what I could eat for the next week. I only came up short that first month. After that, I got better and was able to make the money last for the full month.

After a few months, it occurred to me to get a job. It sounds so silly. Here I was 30 years old and most people would have thought of that step much earlier — but I never had to because I didn't really need it.

The YMCA hired me, and it was wonderful. I ended up loving it there. The Y doesn't pay that much, but they provide a lot of training and it was a great group. That opened the door for me working.

In the meantime, Bill and I had a lot of contact. He was willing to talk to me as much as I wanted to talk. He gave me ideas. Probably the idea of getting a job even came from him.

My father couldn't have picked a better person to fill this role. All in all, Bill and I had a very respectful relationship. He was just the right mix of being firm and being kind. He had a sense of humor. We would joke around a little bit.

After Bill and I had worked for probably a year, I felt like I had grown up and taken charge of my life financially. It was a little late, granted — but at least it happened. I now knew what I spent. I knew how to work under a budget — I was in control. I had a job that I liked. All of it happened within a year, and it all happened because my dad paired me up with this wonderful trust officer.

What was it in me that made this happen? I always had this sense of wanting to have a good life, and a vague sense that it involved taking charge of my life. But I was just kind of in the dark about how and where to start. I don't think I ever would have done what I did with Bill by myself.

The other part of that question is: What was it about Bill that made these changes take place? It was his personality. The role he was playing with me, I think, was well within his job-description. He was very generous with his time and anything I might want to learn. He was very firm about the parameters of the budget. It was just the right mix.

I worked with him for just two or three years overall. The second and third years, we fine-tuned my personal-finance skills; he taught me basics of trusts and banking and how to read my trust statements; and he helped me with a few "sticky wickets" in my YMCA job.

I learned what my father wanted me to learn. I became responsible and stopped overspending. To this day, I'm pretty careful.

That day Dad and I walked to the bank — it was a turning point. It began the time when I grew up financially. That is why I have such good memories of working with Bill.

The transformation in this tale began when the father drew a line — first against his own belief that life for his children should be carefree, and then against functioning as an ATM. Even better: The storyteller was eager to learn and Bill knew what to do.

FROM FLAWED HISTORY TO FRESH START

This one's a little bit like those detective tales where the only course is to stay curious and keep asking why, how and when. The trick is to get past dealing with the effects and see if you can discern one fundamental cause.

On being appointed successor trustee, it seemed wise to interview each of the adult children individually. By using a list of questions, I could better understand what their relationships were with other family members, what they knew about the family company, and what their own financial situation was.

The interviews revealed an undercurrent of negativity with regard to family relationships that was a result of misunderstanding and misinformation about the way the trust had been set up and funded.

Years before my appointment, their father had transferred the family business into trust as a tax-saving strategy. He explained his actions and his reasoning in a handwritten note to his children. His vision was that all of his children would work together in the family business. When the business increased in value substantially more than what had been expected, the trust became the central point of the family's wealth.

The misunderstanding was that some of the children mistakenly thought that they, not the trust, owned the growth in the value of the family business. This was a significant misunderstanding, and it led to a lot of animosity.

One of the siblings periodically communicated the misinformation to family members, giving the impression that the trust was withholding significant amounts of money from them. As a result, some of the children were demoralized and didn't want to be involved with the family. Family members and their advisors were afraid to speak up, to question, and to convey what was on their mind.

Using information from the interviews, it was possible to find a copy of the note written by their father. I talked with each person to reconstruct how the trust had been funded and financed and created a schedule that showed all of the distributions received over the years and the value of the trust. The facts were brought to light.

Having the facts and discussing them, they came to a much better understanding of the trust and their relationship and responsibility to it. As a result of this process, they understood that nothing had been "stolen" from them. In the end, all but one of the children bonded together to comprise a closer and more effective family.

Family meetings were used to increase family involvement. At the meetings we created an environment where everyone felt comfortable asking questions. From their questions we learned the type of information that they needed in order to better understand the situation. We presented the information in a format that was easily understood by the various family members who had different levels of education and understanding about financial matters.

The family came together to agree on new organizational structures for the family business as well as new business ventures.

With the help of a facilitator, we focused on talking about their family's history and values. The participants were very engaged and took over the process themselves. It was an informal process. Some of the children researched the family history and did a family tree to memorialize their history. From that came conversation about the values that had enabled the family to get to the place where they were.

It was an organic process that worked in large part, I think, because they were so relieved that all that misunderstanding that had bothered them in the past had now been cleared up. This freed them to be able to communicate like adults about complex issues. In doing so, they matured as a family.

This maturity showed up in other ways. They were more professional in how they managed the family business, as well as in how they managed the family foundation. They learned who they were and who they wanted to be.

A couple of the children started their own businesses in areas that interested them personally and are doing pretty well. Another child decided that he didn't want to be a businessman. He wanted to dedicate his life to charity and he is doing that.

This had been a difficult project with a lot of risk because, in the beginning, everybody was afraid that it would end up with family members suing each other. The family had the courage to go forward anyway. Once the emotional turmoil was over, they found the strength and the space to live life with the values they held dear for themselves.

My advice to families is to tackle the historical emotional issues within the family because they are an impediment to moving forward with the aspirations and projects that really matter. My advice to trustees is to ask the hard questions while seeking to be a calming influence in the midst of the turmoil.

Once a framework both pervasive and longstanding is swept away, family connectivity and creativity can develop an entirely new structure. Sounds simple — but, in practice, this story is an incremental one where, at times, the "removal" of the original assumptions no doubt felt like defusing explosives. An astonishing amount of positive energy can be released — once the scariest part is over.

THE UNPOPULAR BENEFICIARY

A beneficiary can be so demanding that you, the trustee, find yourself wanting to "make them wrong." When in severe doubt regarding your options or your objectivity, what can be done? What this next storyteller did: Bring in a mentor, supervisor or other experienced colleague.

I was trustee for a very wealthy and extremely dysfunctional family. One of the children, Anne, was a very successful businesswoman who had alienated everybody in the family. Her parents barely spoke to her, and she had nothing to do with her four siblings or her two sons. She had divorced the father of her children and was working on a second marriage.

When I first met Anne, she said her children had been physically abusive to her and were drug-addicts. She warned me about providing them with any funds — because, she assured me, the money would end up being used to buy more drugs.

Anne's trusts were "spray trusts," which meant that not only Anne but also her children were the potential beneficiaries. Anne's mother, the grantor of the trusts, had cautioned me not to rely on Anne to find out what her children were doing because, unfortunately, she didn't think Anne a good parent. She advised me to check directly with the children to evaluate their needs.

That advice was something I took very much to heart. And I was very glad that we had that meeting because the mother died shortly thereafter.

Dealing with Anne, I had heard terrible stories about her children. And when I met separately with them, they told me their mother had cut them off without a penny: "We don't have any way to live; our father doesn't have any money. Will you give us money to live on?"

At my insistence, Anne's children came up with a budget of how they were going to spend what they might receive. Basically, they needed money for rent, and one of them was going to school. I agreed to help them and arranged for direct payment of rent and tuition, with a modest amount paid to each of them directly.

When Anne learned about those arrangements, she was very angry. She thought I was being completely irresponsible by giving these kids money. She was very hostile, and never forgave me for doing so.

At another point, Anne came to me and said her vacation home had been damaged by a hurricane. She wanted money from the trust to help her repair that house. I asked whether she had insurance. She said yes, and the insurance will pay for part of the damage — but not for everything.

I basically didn't like Anne and my immediate reaction was to say no. She had other money, so there was no reason for her to come to the trust.

Then I thought: "Gee, I'm in trouble here because I'm letting my personal feelings interfere — and I really can't do that. This is not the way to behave. There is nothing in the trust that says I have to look at her other resources. In fact, the trust says I should not *consider* her other resources."

I went to my supervisor and told him: "I think I have a problem here. Because I so dislike this woman, I'm automatically saying no."

The supervisor and I talked about the merits of her request. We worked together and concluded that it was perfectly legitimate. She was going to show me the bills for the repairs; she would also show me what she got from insurance. Everything was in place. If I had been neutral, or liked her, there wouldn't have been any difficulty.

We did give her the money and it was the right thing to do.

We began by lauding this storyteller for calling in a more neutral advisor. As for the other half of the story, regarding Anne's grown children: Many situations are not what they seem — yet most every challenge can be figured out. Wherever possible, don't make a decision or lock in a point of view before interacting with every person who will be materially affected by that decision.

FOR THE LOVE OF SIBLINGS

Much is written about the role trustees may play in the lives of beneficiaries starting out in life. Service to elder beneficiaries is far less examined. In this story, a wise trustee understands that each family can be viewed as an emotional system; and therefore a decision for, or with, one individual can't be made without affecting at least some of his or her relatives. Even subtler, in this case, is the fact that a life-change in old age can mean adding happiness and comfort to a "necessary" situation.

This story is about brother and a sister as they age. It's also about a trustee who believes that considering the human needs, not just the financial ones, is very important.

The lead character is the grantor, Bernard, who has no children but is very close to his sibling, Felicia, and her children. And I am the trustee.
At the outset of the story, Felicia is being cared for in her home. Bernard, who is not legally competent, lives in a facility. It isn't easy for either to travel to see the other, and it just doesn't happen. The family's difficult decision to move Felicia to an assisted-living facility is prompting me to think about Bernard — why couldn't he move to the same place?

Learning how important Bernard and Felicia have been to one another takes investigation and questions, but my role as a trustee is about getting deeply involved. I talk with Bernard as well as several of his family members, including one who is his guardian and another the holder of the power of attorney for property; both are caring, interested and involved.

Not only are his family members an important part of Bernard's support system, they are also contingent beneficiaries with interests in Bernard's estate.

Those conversations confirm a gap, a missing piece that will make life better for Bernard, involving his wonderful relationship with his sister. I am hearing details about the importance of family to Bernard and his love for his sister. These talks also confirm the family's desire to reunite the two.

The trust gives me the discretion to do things that benefit Bernard. And I come to believe that one of the things important in administering this trust is reconnecting the siblings. Because they are so fond of each other and enjoy the time they spend together, separate living arrangements is actually a problem I can help end. It's clear to me that this has to be accomplished.

While reuniting a brother and sister may not seem legally relevant, it means a lot to my charge, Bernard. As it happens, the decision to move Bernard is made easier because the new living arrangement is less expensive for him. (Had it been a more difficult situation, I might have gotten some formalized consent from the other stakeholders.)

Now Bernard sees Felicia every day. They are happy to be with each other. It's a thrilling resolution.

It's important to look at a beneficiary's true best interests in the context of their family system. Routinely, when doing due diligence before accepting appointment as trustee, I meet with all the players involved — beneficiaries, family members, guardians, caregivers. I'm joining a team and have to know them well.

I am also careful about getting involved. I want a high confidence level that we as a team can deal with whatever issues come up later. I look to see how open and "awake" the key people are.

The trustee's role is about being aware of a beneficiary's different needs, including serving their families when doing so benefits the beneficiary. As a trustee, make sure you think about how to deal practically, powerfully and proactively within the four corners of the trust document.

When you think of how much sadness and anxiety accompany a family's decision to move an elder into assisted living, the foregoing story has the feel of a minor miracle — we just saw "one plus one" take the place of one minus one.

MONEY ALWAYS HAS A MESSAGE

The captain of this ship — the head of the family — has a clear image of his "motley" crew. Speaking to the trustee, the captain stonewalls on making a tangible gesture of confidence in his adult children, and is otherwise silent. So the trustee and the crew find ways to show the captain: They're not "motley" at all.

This story has to do with the relationship between the patriarch and his three adult children, all of whom had previously received substantial distributions from irrevocable trusts. Year in, year out, we would recommend to the father that he make annual exclusion gifts. The father grumbled and told us "the kids already have too much money."

So we did an analysis from a tax point of view: Three children, 12 grandchildren — and the true financial benefit would be to save taxes for the family. We went through all of that with the patriarch. He acknowledged the math, but kept on grumbling.

Listening to the patriarch, what became clear to the corporate trustee, who was also the family's wealth advisor, was that he didn't think his children had done smart things with the money he'd already given them. He didn't want to give them more because he didn't think they would use it wisely.

In advising each of those children during the next 18 months, we thought a lot about positive things that each adult child was doing in his or her own life. With their permission — absolutely necessary due to confidentiality — we included in quarterly meetings a family update of anywhere between one and three bullet points of financial decisions or actions completed by each adult during the past period of time. The list might include refinancing a mortgage, setting up or contributing to an IRA, reducing their level of spending, developing a budget — whatever we could think of.

In short, we focused on the next generation's financial accomplishments. Useful ones, not just busy work.

That next Christmas we got calls from each of the adult kids, in tears, saying "Dad loves me." What does that mean? "Well, Dad trusts me." And what makes you say that? "He gave me a big holiday check."

Recall this old phrase: "It is never just the money, it is the money and the message." By withholding annual gifts, Dad had been sending a message that he didn't trust or love them. What he suddenly gave them — and it was never about the money, as they didn't need it — was a vote of confidence and, yes, his love.

That was a miracle to me. Took almost three years to bring about, and it really changed their dynamics. There were also collateral benefits in terms of a father in old age and the kids being available for him. Very gratifying.

This story explains itself, yes?

CHAPTER FIVE:
WISE DECISION-MAKERS

In the prior chapter, we saw Trustscapers initiate positive change. Now here's our challenge to you, the reader...

Think of rough patches involving your own trustscape — and select one that turned out well. Describe that episode as a positive story with a beginning, middle, and end (much like those you're reading here). What was it about you, the others, or the circumstances that contributed to success?

Now we're moving from rough patches to innovative trustees that, when asked to make unorthodox distributions, "stretch" to reach the right outcome without sending the wrong message.

TAXES CAN MAKE YOU SICK

Over time, the wise trustee will refine his or her ability to think of novel and productive ways to address a knotty problem and make the "right" decision. And here you'll see a wise trustee in action.

Susan was an alcoholic and had been declared incompetent. As her trustee, I met her after she had gone to court to have herself declared competent. (That's not something I had ever heard of before, or for that matter since.)

Susan had stopped drinking and was now in Alcoholics Anonymous. She was the beneficiary of two trusts, one under the will of each parent. The trust under her father's will provided only for distributions of income. The trust under her mother's will provided for income distributions and, in addition, principal payments — but only for medical reasons.

There was no other reason that we could give money to Susan — either directly, or on her behalf.

I liked Susan very much. I thought: "Here is a woman who has struggled all of her life and is trying very hard to pull her life together."

One day she called me and was almost hysterical.

"What's the matter, Susan?"

"I'm going to go to jail."

"What do you mean you are going to go to jail? Why are you going to jail?"

"The IRS is after me. I forgot to pay my taxes."

Other than the trusts, she had no resources. She had no savings and no job. She didn't know what she was going to do. "Could the trusts help me?" She also mentioned the temptation to start drinking again.

Susan was under the care of a psychiatrist who told her that she had to resolve her tax problem because her anxiety was becoming worse.

I thought about the situation. Maybe we had a way to say that her failure to pay taxes was making her dangerously ill. Maybe we could say that the payment of her tax debt was, for all intents and purposes, a medical expense.

"Would it be all right if I spoke with your psychiatrist?" I told her why. Susan replied: "Yes, you may do that."

The psychiatrist said that pressure from the IRS was the immediate, and just about the only, topic on Susan's mind. Susan couldn't think beyond it and it was interfering with her recovery, specifically her ability to stay sober. So here was an awful situation.

The psychiatrist readily agreed to write a letter to me confirming that Susan's tax situation was worsening her medical situation. That was a help.

On the basis of that letter and my understanding of Susan's plight, I agreed to pay her outstanding taxes and obtained the necessary approvals within the Trust Company to do so. We then paid her outstanding taxes. We also set up a system to reserve a certain amount of her trust income to pay future taxes so she wouldn't face this problem again.

I wondered: "Why did her mother limit the trust's ability to pay for anything other than medical purposes?" I concluded that she was worried that, if Susan got her hands on the money, she would drink it, or waste it in some other way. But I don't think she would have wanted Susan to be negatively impacted due to an inability to pay taxes.

Giving Susan the money to pay taxes was the right decision. This all worked because I knew Susan and asked permission to talk to her psychiatrist.

The easy answer would have been "no." But this trustee, like many others among our storytellers, went beyond "easy." To help resolve a beneficiary's predicament, he gave weight to what the trust-creator logically would have intended.

JAMES HAS A THIRST FOR EDUCATION

A very productive era in American-Russian relations began in 1985 when one side adopted the maxim "trust but verify." That same principle saves the day here, except that we're headed to Paris rather than Moscow.

L et me start off with reminding you that my career was spent at XYZ Trust Company. I frequently dealt with discretionary trusts for which the Trust Company served as the sole trustee. In my role as a trust officer of those trusts, I was essentially deciding whether we would exercise our discretion to provide funds to the requesting beneficiary.

For situations in which the requested amount exceeded a certain total or percentage of the trust principal, we had in place procedures requiring me to obtain the approval of senior officers. To make sure that the document was being complied with, and risks were being assessed properly, there was always a second set of eyes. I can't remember being overruled in any such situation.

Many of these trusts empowered the trustee to exercise absolute discretion without any limitations; and some provided very general standards, such as for education or general welfare. A great deal of responsibility was being exercised very carefully.

It was the Trust Company's philosophy that, when discretion was provided for in the document, you had to view it as a positive tool in your relationship with the beneficiary. In other words, the tendency was: "Well, how can we respond affirmatively? If we can't give you exactly what you want, in the way that you want it, how can we work it out so you still get what is beneficial to you?" Perhaps the best example is a beneficiary by the name of James.

James was part of a very wealthy family that had a family office. The head of the family office was the individual trustee, with the Trust Company as co-trustee. The head of the family office had a very long history with James, and it was quite negative. He did not trust him, he didn't like him, and James knew it.

James was the type of person who never had enough money. He was careless with his spending and was always thinking of very creative ways of getting money beyond the trust income to which he was entitled.

One day James called. He was in his late thirties and living most of the time in Paris. He told me: "I want to go back to school. I want to get a postgraduate degree at the Sorbonne. There is a program that I like very much and it will take about two years to complete. Completion will enable me to have a better life, and maybe become a teacher. I don't know what I want to do specifically, but this program will provide career choices I won't otherwise have. It's something I really want to do."

I spoke to the individual trustee and he said, "Absolutely not. First of all, we don't make principal distributions from our trusts, no matter what the document says. And secondly — and most important — I don't trust James."

Not only did James' trust provide broad discretion for payments to him from principal, but the document specifically said that we could invade principal for education. The individual trustee replied: "How do we know he is really going to use the money for that purpose?"

The problem the individual trustee had was that he couldn't conceive of James having changed. I had a different take. I really thought he was serious about this postgraduate endeavor. Because I had not known him as long as the other trustee had, there wasn't a negative history between James and me.

We worked out the following and presented it to James: We would give him the money to pay for his education over a two-year period. Since we did not want to be involved in paying his individual bills, he would have to give us an estimate of his total educational expenses, including a breakdown of those costs. Once we agreed to that amount, we would pay him in quarterly installments. He would have to budget accordingly so that when he got a payment at the beginning of the quarter, he could not expect to come back a month later and say that he needed extra money.

In addition to that, we wanted to make sure that he was indeed registered at the Sorbonne. So we required certification from the Sorbonne attesting to the fact that he is officially registered there, and also required that the certification be updated every six months. Part of his program required James to submit a thesis. We wanted periodic reports from his thesis director — not details, but enough to know he was making satisfactory progress.

On those conditions, we would give him the money to proceed. James said "sure." He came back with a budget. We had concerns and problems.

For example, to fulfill the Sorbonne's requirement that he be fluent in languages other than English and French, he wanted to spend six months in Madrid to learn Spanish. Accordingly, his preliminary budget included the rental of a flat for that period. We said that he didn't have to go to Madrid to learn Spanish; he could hire a tutor in Paris and only the cost of that tutor would be covered.

James was upset about certain things the trustees required and the trustees thought he was over-reacting when he objected. But finally he said: "Okay. I'm willing to do these things because I'm really serious about it."

We finally reached a negotiated agreement and it worked out fine.

Of course, from time to time James called to say he was running short that quarter. Could I advance him funds? I would help him out, but only after we established that he was indeed still enrolled at the Sorbonne and also getting satisfactory comments from the thesis director. At the end of the two years, he got his degree. He really came through.

Subsequently, I met him a few times while in Paris. He was now a serious person who really wanted to move on to a different stage in his life. And he showed his trustees a real interest in learning and succeeding.

I thought that was a very creative way of responding to somebody's legitimate needs, dealing with a very difficult co-trustee and, frankly, a very difficult beneficiary. I consider this a very successful story.

Trust but verify? "Verification," to be effective, sometimes has to be broken down into incremental actions and checkpoints. A few can misfire, and the transformation still be achieved.

PHILOSOPHY YES, RIGIDITY NO

This trustee begins with a well-developed philosophical point of view — and is able to hold to it, yet change his mind. How? By allowing his professional advisor and mentor to ask questions that help redefine the situation. The trustee's decision changes — or at least doesn't go where he first thought it would — even as his point of view stays intact.

This story starts with a firm policy on distributions to family members as beneficiaries of the family trusts. As trustee, the principle I have always followed is that individual family members have to make their own way. Whatever standard of living, or whatever economic level they achieve, has to be a result of their own efforts.

The family trust funds are to be used only in two circumstances — for an upside, or to deal with a downside. "Upside" means interesting and productive opportunities — not necessarily a business or financial opportunity, but endeavors that are beneficial to the individual. The "downside" would be catastrophes that an individual with typical financial resources would be unable to handle on his or her own.

In between those extremes, the standard of living has to be taken care of by the beneficiaries, at whatever level it turns out to be.

This policy has been impressed on the family members countless times. They don't necessarily like it, but they have reluctantly accepted it. And I figured the policy would not be difficult to adhere to.

A while back my niece Elizabeth called me and, rather nervously, asked: "Would funds be available for me to hire a cleaning lady for my house? I am very busy and having one less burden would be of great benefit."

My first internal reaction was "obviously not," because hiring a cleaning woman is clearly a standard-of-living factor — a subsidy — that she should take care of herself. Before giving Elizabeth my answer, however, I said to her: "Let me give this some consideration..."

Puzzled and troubled by the request, I felt my answer would have to be no. But before deciding, I reached out to my mentor. I wanted some advice, comfort, and — hopefully — someone to agree with me.

He responded by saying, "Let's look at this a little more closely" — and then he asked some questions about Elizabeth.

"Does she work full-time?" "Yes."

"Does she have two young sons she has to raise?" "Yes."

"Is her husband fully occupied with his job?" "Yes."

"How much time does she have for herself, in light of all of these other things she has to do?" My guess — a good guess — was "very little."

My mentor then said, "Well, under those circumstances, Elizabeth is obviously very busy and having a cleaning lady come in once a week would give her a little free time to sit back and relax; to think about this, that and the other thing; to unwind. Would you consider that having this little time for herself to be an enhancement or a subsidy?"

Note how my mentor did not draw a conclusion or give me a direct answer. Instead, he asked these few questions and, by doing so, recast the situation.

That process led me to the conclusion that hiring a cleaning woman would be a true enhancement and not a subsidy. The few extra hours a week of free time could really make significant improvements in the quality of Elizabeth's life. Although it initially looked like a subsidy, in Elizabeth's world, it would be an enhancement.

Under my policy, therefore, the funds should be provided and they were, from a now enlightened and clear-conscienced me. Elizabeth expressed her appreciation.

Though still the family curmudgeon and spoilsport, I can, occasionally, learn something. In this instance, I learned not to be simplistic.

My ordinary approach is to look at things in black and white, but doing so isn't always appropriate. Some situations, on the surface, appear to be black and white — but they require more careful thought. They can turn out to be quite different from what I, or you, with our own views, first imagine.

So — I learned to be somewhat more flexible. And I give the major credit to my mentor. Without that conversation, the automatic decision would have been, "This is just something that Elizabeth ought to pay for herself," and an opportunity for enhancement of the life of one of my family members would have been lost.

This storyteller knows why viewing a surprise proposal "in black and white...isn't always appropriate." But turning to a mentor who asks robust questions and broadens perspective, hardly ever fails. As trustee, have you developed philosophical guidelines? Not an ideology, and not snap judgments, but guidelines that are well thought through?

A CHILDHOOD DREAM FULFILLED

One can read this next story and get sidetracked by the bold nature of the request. In fact, the principle followed by both the trustee and family member is about as conservative — and as down to earth — as you will find. See if you can deduce it before the storyteller reaches the end.

This story involves Peter, the husband of my niece Sarah. From the time he was a boy, Peter had an ambition to be a pilot, to fly a plane. Different from the typical childhood ambition, this stayed with him.

At one point, Sarah called and told me about Peter's ambition — dream, passion — to fly a plane and asked whether funds would be available for him to take flying lessons. I think she expected me to say no.

This was not an easy request. In various ways it was unusual. It was not inexpensive; there would be no economic benefit; and some real physical risks were attached to it.

Sarah's request on behalf of Peter was an instance where, on the face of it, one would say: "This is a luxury, how can you justify it? It's also risky. What if Peter has an accident while flying and Sarah ends up being a widow?"

I asked Sarah, "Are you comfortable with this, and are you willing to take the risks?" She said yes to both.

I said I would think about it. I did. It seemed to me that this would be an enhancement — something very important to Peter, or it wouldn't have stayed with him all these years.

However, I remained concerned about the risks. So I asked if they had adequate insurance in the event of an accident. The answer was yes.

I called and spoke to Sarah's mother, Mary. The funds would be coming from Mary's portion of the family assets and therefore I needed her permission as well as her approval. I asked whether she was comfortable with Peter taking flying lessons and, in addition, pointed out that she would be paying for it.

Mary is, after all, both a mother and a mother-in-law. One would anticipate that she would have all types of concerns. She did have some — but she surprised me by saying that this project was okay with her.

I did want to be sure that Peter had carefully checked out the flying school to make sure it was competent. I had some other due-diligence things I wanted done and they were.

Finally I said: "All right, we will provide the funds for the flying lessons," and we did. After an extended period of training, Peter got his private pilot's license.

Despite the unusual circumstances, and a request that didn't fit what one would typically think of as an enhancement, for me the important and overriding issue was that this avocation was a long-term passion of his; it was something he had dreamed of doing since childhood.

I felt, and still feel, that helping family members fulfill dreams, even the unusual one like getting a pilot's license, is properly part of the mandate.

As part of his deliberation, what the trustee did is as mundane as it is important: Converse with everyone who matters.

DOES ANYBODY REALLY NEED A HELICOPTER?

This story, offering more than its share of improbable imagery, shows our readers who are beneficiaries that their own dilemmas and requests are not as "out of this world" as they might think.

I always thought it very helpful to know the person who set up the trust — or the lawyer who drafted the governing instrument — to try to understand the grantor's intentions regarding the trustee's discretion in making distributions.

95

And, if I didn't know the grantor or the lawyer, perhaps something could be found in the file indicating how that discretion should be exercised. We didn't always have that at the Trust Company. Sometimes trusts had been in existence for quite a long while and there were no records in the file containing such insights into the grantor's thinking.

The story I'm about to tell you is one where I do know the grantor. She is still alive and is a friend of mine.

Marie, the grantor, set up trusts for each of her three children. One of them is for her son Jack. Marie and Jack live in a third-world country. Jack is a businessman who is involved in numerous enterprises that take him to various parts of his country.

He called me one day and said, "I'm really getting concerned about my safety when driving to various places. Some of these places are very far away. Because the road conditions are so awful, I'm away from my family for long periods of time. The roads are also dangerous — with frequent carjackings and kidnappings. Sometimes it takes 10 hours to get to a place, so I have to stay over and be away from my family."

Then Jack lifted my sights — literally. "I've thought a lot about this and I would like to buy a helicopter. I can't afford the purchase on my own and I'll need help from the trust."

My first reaction was: "You must be kidding." Upon reflection, I could certainly understand the logic of his request. Yet there was no shortage of side issues.

I asked: "How are you going to pay for the upkeep of the helicopter if you get one? What about the insurance and the fuel? Are you going to be the only person piloting it? Will you need a crew?"

He replied: "I don't want the trust to pay for all of the costs of the helicopter — I don't think that would be right. I have some money of my own that I'm willing to put towards it, and I could borrow some money for the purchase price as well as the upkeep. That would still not be enough for me to do this on my own, which is why I need some help from the trust."

Jack's case began to be a compelling one. He had genuine safety concerns. Driving on the roads where he is can be very, very dangerous. I know how devoted he is to his family and how he hates being away from them.

I also know that when Marie created the trust, and asked me to be the trustee, she wanted me to be liberal in making distributions. In addition to including very broad discretionary powers in the trust document, she provided a letter of intent, emphasizing that the trustee should exercise discretion as though Jack had the property outright. That's quite a powerful statement as to how the trustee is to be guided in considering a principal distribution.

I also knew that Marie had a great deal of confidence in Jack and that he was a very sound person. So I said: "Once I'm assured that you will be able to take care of the upkeep, the insurance, and other expenses, that would be fine — but I think you have some other really personal issues on this."

He asked, "Like what? If you mean my mother, I've spoken to her and she agrees with me." I replied: "Actually, I wasn't thinking so much about your mother. I am really thinking of your siblings, who will find out that you have acquired a helicopter." (This is a family that has been very modest in the way they display or spend their wealth.)

"Although it is not important to tell them where you got the money, I think they will all conclude that you got it from the trust. You ought to be prepared for how they are going to regard you and how they might treat this. Are you prepared to deal with that? Acquiring a helicopter could create some issues for you. Are you ready to deal with these potential sibling issues?"

"I can deal with it," Jack said. "I think they will understand why I want to have a copter. I plan to let them know."

I had already decided that he should get the money for the helicopter, particularly since he was partnering with the trust — that is, it impressed me that he would come up with money from his own resources and then borrow for the purchase and upkeep. It showed a seriousness of purpose.

So, Jack did get the helicopter — and his siblings, much to my surprise, gave him no difficulty with it at all. No doubt they recognized how difficult an environment he was living and working in.

Give kudos to the storyteller for (a) reminding us of the critical role of discerning the trust-creator's intentions, and (b) reminding "Jack" that sibling displeasure could be stirred. In the end, it wasn't — but our storyteller was properly thorough at every step.

WE ALL FELT LIKE GODPARENTS

Are there ways to creatively support a beneficiary and her family that were not contemplated when the trust was originally created? More times than we imagine, someone will bring that question to the forefront.

Grandmother had set up a trust for two generations of income beneficiaries: Daughter and Daughter's children (Granddaughter and Grandson). When Granddaughter and Grandson are both deceased, the trust will come to an end and what is left will be divided among their children.

The discretionary provision for Daughter was limited to medical — and that was it. The discretionary provision for distributions to Granddaughter and Grandson was much broader, something similar to "maintenance, education and general welfare" but, interestingly, did not mention medical or health.

Granddaughter and her husband had been trying unsuccessfully for years to have children. She came to the trust for funding of in-vitro fertilization.

Our analysis covered many angles. Would that come under maintenance and general welfare? Who would object to an accounting of such a distribution? What would Grandmother have wanted with her trust fund that she created for her daughter and grandchildren? Were there ways to creatively think of benefitting the family that weren't contemplated when the trust was originally created? What is the benefit to the family for making such a distribution and what is the potential risk to the trustee?

Grandson was not going to have children, so great-grandchildren who might be brought into being as a result of in-vitro fertilization paid for by the distribution would be the only ones to receive what is left when the trust ends. Isn't that a wonderful thought!

We made the distribution. Granddaughter had children and, as trustees, we all felt like godparents. It was really quite wonderful for the family.

My point is to analyze the trust instrument considering whatever information is available about what the creator might have decided had they still been able to make that decision. What was the family "philosophy"? We might not have had it recorded, but what did we know anecdotally? What can be deduced from all we see and hear?

As a corporate fiduciary, think about what the documents say and what the risks are, and try to avoid saying "no" as the easy answer. Think through why a distribution might be, in fact, valuable.

Most every family has a philosophy — a set of values. But generations can pass with philosophy and values "sitting beneath the surface" and rarely being articulated. As a beneficiary you might, in effect, challenge your trustee to discern that set of values. Once surfaced, a path for more informed decision-making might be revealed.

CHAPTER SIX:
TRUSTSCAPES THAT ENDURE

Some would say the trustees in the just-concluded chapter thought outside the box. We think otherwise. We say that these trustees knew the "box" so well they could comfortably remain within its four corners the entire time — while expanding the box!

And how did they do that? For one thing, they were master craftsmen deploying skills honed over time. But more importantly — and this is the key — they were shining examples of favoring "qualitative" over "quantitative" well beyond the threshold three-to-one ratio.

Which brings up a question: Why would anyone want to be a trustee? For trustees who are family members (and some trust officers, for that matter), it's all about the future of the family. It's a real service at the most basic level.

You've seen it time and again in the positive stories. For example, trustees who recognize that their responsibility is to provide opportunities, sometimes small and sometimes big, for beneficiaries to become more mature.

If you want a challenge and want to make a difference, this is the place to do it. Will it be easy? No. Is it necessary? Yes — it is.

This final array of stories illustrates the positive effect of Trustscapers remaining engaged, creative, and persevering over time — and in the process learning something about the other and about self.

GOING BEYOND EASY

This is about making a commitment without realizing how difficult the fulfillment might one day be. And then, after perceiving the roughness of the trail, going the extra mile to make it work. As difficult as that proves to be — "She was rather eccentric, and still is" — getting to know the beneficiary is what makes it possible to genuinely assist her.

I was in public accounting practice in 1995 when a client asked if I'd be willing to be successor trustee of a trust for his mentally disabled daughter, Susan, upon his death.

I agreed. And, when he died 10 years later, I was appointed trustee.

Not until her father's memorial service did I actually meet Susan. But her relatives had painted not a pretty picture. It seems that a lot of people were afraid of her. At that point, she was in her forties. She was rather eccentric, and still is.

Susan lives alone with her two cats. She is covered under SSI (the part of the Social Security program that covers the disabled), has Medicaid coverage for her medical care, and Section 8 subsidized housing for where she lives. When I began working with her as trustee, I had to learn the government rules because I was not permitted to pay anything that would jeopardize her government benefits — food, housing, and the medical expenses not covered by Medicaid.

Sometimes she would be quite agitated, anxious and aggressive over the phone. At other times, she would be depressed and remorseful for things she might have said. In the early days, on a number of occasions, she committed herself to a local mental facility.

She was quite upset with her father's death and, prior to that, her mother's death. Late one night, extremely depressed and in a morose state, she left a voicemail. Her question was whether I had ever heard her parents say that they loved her. By the time I got back to her, she had forgotten this call and was concerned about other things.

Early on, I tried to emphasize to Susan that we needed to work together as partners because I didn't know what her needs were, and was just learning the ropes on what Medicaid covered. It was important that she understood that I could not okay some of the things she wanted me to accommodate with what she believed to be "her money." Helping her see this required time and a constant, consistent presence.

Sometimes, when overwhelmed by her emotions, Susan needed time to calm down, regain perspective, and understand that her situation wasn't all that bad. Reaching that understanding is where we first connected and started to work well together. As these episodes mounted, I began to remind her — at the outset of each one — that we had been through this before; it was hard, very hard; but she would get through it just like times before. And, she has.

Over the past five or six years our relationship has improved and I believe her condition has improved. Only rarely do I have to remind her that the money in the trust is not her money. Rather, it's her parents' money put in my hands to provide for her needs — to enhance her life beyond what she would otherwise have.

These days, Susan calls two or three times a week (at a minimum) about something that she needs, or something she's upset about, or sometimes just to talk. She knows that I am very busy with other responsibilities. When she calls, she almost always asks if this is a good time to talk and, even better, has organized her thoughts on paper.

If there's a lot going on for her, we might talk every day. I have learned to mostly listen. With the proper conversation, she can begin to understand what's involved, and often we come to the same conclusion.

Since I'm not available on a moment's notice, we have developed systems to address her day-to-day needs. With on-line banking and a Wal-Mart gift card that I can reload on the computer, she obtains the items she needs once I approve. She makes a list of what she would like to purchase. She sends me receipts to match up with what I see on-line.

Occasionally, a Starbucks coffee appears when impulsive buying gets the better of her, but nothing of any consequence. She sends other invoices for me to pay by mail. The Internet generally, and on-line banking especially, have been great resources.

We live about an hour apart by car. I visit Susan a few times a year to make sure her home is habitable and clean. We have developed a routine. I pick her up and we go shopping at Costco for the things she needs that I cannot get shipped on-line from other stores. We go for lunch, then head back to her apartment to unload our purchases and spend a little time talking. These visits have become a chance for relaxed conversation about what's going on in each of our lives.

I think it's important to be able to do things for other people. Involving Susan in a process of doing things for me — for example, getting the receipts together — has given her a sense of doing something for someone else, which has been significant.

She often wants the trust to make extravagant gifts to her sister, nieces or friends. Once we discuss the meaning of making a gift and the messages it can send, she realizes she can make something or write a card and it will mean as much or more than a thing that she cannot afford.

Sometimes, along with the receipts, she'll slip in a note telling me something she wants me to know about her life. This morning a note arrived that said, "Thank you for all the help over the years. I'm grateful to have you on my side. Take care, Susan." Things like this make me feel like I am making a difference. I believe that I have served her and the trust well. She expresses her appreciation a lot more now than she has in the past.

I'm conscious of my role as her trustee and not her friend, which makes for an unusual situation where I have to keep a certain distance. At the same time, she is a big part of my life. I have tried to be a consistent presence in her life and maintain a positive outlook on what we can accomplish together.

This experience has, in certain ways, been a rollercoaster. When we started, I had no idea how to deal with someone who had so few social skills and who reacted with volatility and anger. Every call was a challenge. The person on the other end of the phone was not able to make sense. It was like talking to a crazy person.

Today, she seems much better off emotionally. I did not expect to wind up with such a positive response from our work together and had been braced to have to persist with little progress. But her emotional situation is more stable and she seems happier. When I call her now, nine times out of 10, she is upbeat.

Growing up, I had examples of parents who always found time to work for the benefit of others, especially their children but also friends and strangers. Service to others was expected — not because it was a duty or a responsibility, but because of what you get out of it in terms of feeling personally rewarded. Growing older, I could see the wisdom of this. Being of service is not a selfless act; it has great personal benefits, such as the card from Susan that I mentioned earlier.

Looking to the future, I am concerned about how I will find someone who will take care of Susan and not shut her out when she needs someone to talk to. Being a trustee is not for everyone. I feel I can argue authentically for the existence of individuals whose passion and dreams are in serving others and I believe that when the time comes, I will know how to find them.

This tale illustrates a couple of core points. First, a trustee's obligation goes beyond money-distribution and risk-management. Knowing your beneficiary (and knowing yourself) makes it possible to move from trepidation to appreciation and genuinely assist him or her. And second, a great trustee is looking for his or her successor from the moment he or she takes on the role. Some say that this is a new trustee's highest responsibility.

THE OLDEST OF NINE, THE PATIENCE TO KNOW

Unexpectedly thrust into the role of trustee of her father's trust, our storyteller is determined to find a way through a minefield of complexity and family entanglements. The benefits are not only financial — what they'll save in litigation fees — but what they gain as family participants.

My father was a very successful commercial real-estate developer who amassed quite a fortune. By the time he retired, he owned several construction companies in different parts of the country.

He married five times and had nine children. My mother was his first wife and also his longest wife. I was the first child born of that marriage, which makes me the oldest of his nine children.

My father spent a lot of money supporting his wives. He was also generous with his children — so long as we gave him a good reason why we needed money. But he wasn't forthcoming with where it would go after he died. We knew he had set up a trust, but we didn't know what it said — and would have felt like "moneygrubbers" had we asked him.

The one thing we did know was that anytime he got mad at one of us, he would take that person out of the trust, and let everybody know about it. This was his pattern.

I spent years trying to stay close to my siblings, and it wasn't easy. My father wanted each of us to himself. So, every time we tried to get connected, he would get mad. Nevertheless, I showed up at all the important family events and made sure to call my father at least once a month.

In about 1994, my father gave the majority shares of his largest construction company to my brother Mike. Mike paid for the shares by giving our father a salary.

Ten years later, another brother, James, was running one of my father's other construction companies. Dad still owned it and was driving James crazy by bossing him around. I said to James, "Look, you either get out and do something you want, or buy the company from Dad." He agreed. In the end, he did buy it from our father.

Around the time James purchased the company, it became clear to me that my father wasn't quite right. He had been a very organized man. But now bills weren't getting paid and his papers were no longer organized. He was diagnosed with early-stage dementia.

At this point, my father was not married. Because he wasn't able to live on his own, we hired a caregiver. One of my younger sisters and I flew in regularly. We went through Dad's papers and paid his bills.

In the process, we came across his trust agreement. Almost everything he owned was held in the trust. The trust would terminate at his death and his assets would be distributed. My father was the trustee. And I had been named successor trustee even though never having seen this document.

The trust had been changed over the years — what my sister and I had found was the seventh version. The trust read that James would inherit the company — the enterprise he had already purchased — and nothing else.

My youngest sister would be completely disinherited. At the time he created this version of the trust, my father was probably having a fight with her. And I knew that, if he left it that way, the result would be more family discord, and maybe lawsuits.

My father asked me to step in as trustee and take over for him. He said he believed in me and that I was capable. I knew this role would be hard but, if I didn't do it, it would lead to more emotional turmoil among my siblings. Someone had to take charge of this chaos and I believed I was more capable than the others he was considering.

All the same, I wasn't sure what to do. A lot of mistrust and acrimony had built up among some of my siblings. Some thought that the sister who was left out of the trust shouldn't get a share because she didn't have much to do with our father. The reason she didn't have much to do with him was because he usually refused to talk with her when she did anything that he did not agree with.

Several of us raised the matter with our father. "Look, Daddy, here's the way your trust reads, and I don't think you really mean this for our sister. Also, James has already bought his inheritance — another big problem with this document." My father said, "Yeah, yeah, you're right." Those of us present agreed that the trust should be changed.

We found a lawyer who had been doing this kind of thing for his entire career. He was a wonderful man. Three of my siblings and my father joined me in meeting with him. We presented our situation and gave him a copy of the trust. We explained the changes we wanted and why.

The lawyer took my father into another room, separate from the rest of us, to satisfy himself of my father's competence to make decisions. He asked my father if he wanted to make the changes. Dad told the lawyer "yes" and the changes were made.

After the meeting with the lawyer, I detailed the changes to those of my siblings who had not been present — explaining why they would be getting less as a result of the changes. Most were okay with that.

At the time we met with the lawyer, my father was about six months from his dementia reaching the point where he would no longer be capable of making decisions of this nature. As his cognitive abilities declined, he was diagnosed with Alzheimer's. We moved him to assisted living.

Serving as his trustee kept me amazingly involved with him. It became a full-time job. I cut back on my practice as a family therapist and, according to my father's wishes, paid myself a small stipend from the trust to make up for the time being spent on his affairs.

As far as his financial life was concerned, I essentially became my father and tried to act as I thought he would have when he was at his best — I wanted to honor his best self. He had raised us to be that way. By doing so, I rose to my best self.

This was a complicated family situation because he was supporting several of his ex-wives — one of whom had considerable medical expenses — and one of my sisters was still in college. Sometimes I had to say no to requests from siblings, and rework their relationships with our father's money. I tried to be kind about it.

My father lived for four years after Alzheimer's was diagnosed. During that time, I made new connections with my siblings. This never would have happened had he not lived those final four years. My sense of Dad was broadened because they knew history about him that I didn't.

All kinds of stories were exchanged. I never knew my youngest sister very well (the one who had been disinherited prior to amending the trust). Now in her twenties, she had been born when I was in my thirties. Being trustee served as an entrée to a relationship with her: Now I knew stuff about her and she knew stuff about me. We traveled together to visit our brother Mike after his son was born. When my sister saw the baby, she burst into tears because she finally felt like she was part of the family.

There were some surprises. I learned that Mike, whom I'd known as a bundle of complications, has a great sense of humor. I watched videotapes of him as a child and he was hilarious. I learned that another of my brothers is a poet. Stories were tying us together.

I also saw this as a big opportunity to create relationships with some of the ex-wives — different from the impressions I had of them from my father. There hadn't been opportunities to do this before. If I had tried, my father would get mad and would keep me apart not only from his wives but also their kids.

As my father's condition deteriorated, I intended to ask each of my siblings to prepare a eulogy talking about what our father had meant to them. He died suddenly, before I had the opportunity to make this request.

So I gave the eulogy at my father's funeral, blessing each of his children with words he might have said. You could have heard a pin drop. Something seemed to free up — a feeling of peace and possibility. That really reset things for me, and led to the realization that I could have a relationship with each of these people.

After the funeral, we held a reception at Mike's house. Everyone attended, including children, grandchildren and ex-wives. For most of us, the time together was happy and inclusive. We took a group photo. The tension in some quarters, however, was pretty high: Anxiety around our father's death was being channeled into money issues. I knew I needed to get the trust distributed as soon as possible.

The burial was in my father's hometown in Montana, where he had felt most attached. The trust paid travel costs for his children who wanted to be there. That was important because it enabled us to visit places that are part of our legacy and tell story after story about our father's life. We were all grateful for the time together.

The next morning, a blizzard set in. One of my brothers ranched in the area. We all pitched in to help him herd his cattle. We were bound together in a noncompetitive way. The barriers that had been between us were further broken down. It was poetry.

My siblings and I live in different parts of the country. When our father was alive, we visited him at different times and were not very connected to each other. The money we inherited has allowed us to visit each other and connect in ways that we could not previously. Today there is far less hostility and emotional cutoff.

Taking on this kind of complexity has been emotional for us, but well worth it. I think the experience helped us all to grow up — to live with differences while at the same time connecting over the essential fact that we all share a legacy.

With the patriarch's failing powers and the related distribution of wealth, the need for calm connection and problem-solving increased. One person in a family who is willing to place the events in a broader context, relate to each person (yes, even the most distant) and not "take sides" can, in time, provide a sense of family unity and cooperation.

A TRUSTAFARIAN ADVISES

Over the years, a trustee and beneficiary working together can be a strong influence on the beneficiary's process of maturing. This storyteller's trustee met him where he was, saw "an individual separate and apart from everyone," and together, beneficiary and trustee laid a foundation for developing "trust that I still have today."

I was 22 years old when my grandmother passed away and left an inheritance to my siblings and myself. Until that point, I hadn't had a trust fund but I certainly knew what it was all about: You get money each month on a certain date, which means you use it all up in the next 30 days — and then stress-out until the next remittance comes.

At least that's what I witnessed some of those in my family who did have trust funds do on a regular basis. It certainly didn't seem that wonderful to me at the time — too much stress!

Living at home with my mother, I thought I was doing just fine. I already had an undergraduate degree and was working in a field where I was making a small living for myself — new car, terrific girlfriend, and a few bucks in my pocket — partying and going to concerts, playing music and living a glorious life. (Unlike most of my distraught siblings waiting for their monthlies to come in, I got paid in cash weekly.)

After the funeral we met at my grandmother's law firm. I was the first one there. I had an impromptu meeting with the attorney that one of my brothers had retained to represent us. He introduced himself. He was probably the nicest man I had ever met. I thought to myself, "He's a lawyer?" This "gentle-man" was not like the lawyers from TV or film but he certainly was stronger in stature, compassion and kindness than all of them put together. (And anyone who has met Jay Hughes, even for a minute, knows just what I mean!)

After a few minutes of talking, I realized he was a terrific teacher. No question that I posed was stupid or too simple. He answered each question I asked and treated me well. I felt safe.

Soon after this, the family showed up — and I sat back to "watch the show." There were several of us and I was the youngest. The others already had trusts for their adult lives but, as mentioned, I didn't have one.

At the reading of the will, my grandmother's lawyer said a lot of stuff in "legalese" that sounded like humming or white noise — until he uttered a series of powerful life-changing words: "The current trusts will be liquidated, sold off, and all the money will go to charity."

Dramatic pause — I thought to myself, "Did he just say what I *think* he said?" As I looked around the conference table at my siblings, their faces slowly dropped to the floor, and I thought: "Welcome to my world, guys!"

The lawyer paused after losing his place (you couldn't make this up!) and everybody was looking around at one another as if to say, "Now what, now what?!" My poor siblings must have thought they were in the poorhouse. I felt bad for about a second or two — okay, I'll be honest: It was more like a millisecond.

The lawyer continued. Finally, he got to a paragraph stating that "new trusts will be established worth such-and-such." All of my siblings sat back in their seats with great sighs of relief. I'd never seen my "cool" siblings sweat so much.

That's when I stopped for a second, doing a fast-rewind to what the lawyer had said not two minutes before — that the new trusts were for "all of the children." That meant I'd be getting money, which meant I wouldn't have to live my life the same way anymore.

I was in a state of shock at that point, only to soon realize: "Now I am one of them. Wait! How much did he say we'd be getting???" (It was a fair amount of money, folks — more than a penny, less than the national debt!)

I was now a "Trustafarian." Any Trustafarian knows that you should always hide your true identity to the world or else be labeled — even by your closest friends — in some offensive way because you'd never have to work or know the pain of financial normalcy.

Society does not look well upon the fortunate. I watched a judge on a reality television show once chastise a defendant who was clearly a Trustafarian (she lived well, wasn't working, and said the magic words "I attend college to learn more and better myself"). The judge gave her "that look" and said something to the effect of "so you're a trust-fund baby...a lazy bum...don't say another word!"

So any Trustafarian knows how to explain to others how and why we live the way we live without saying "rich," coming up with all kinds of reasons. Such as: I did really well on my investments. I got a break on my tax returns. I saved some money up from my last (imaginary) job so I could go back to school and focus... Meanwhile we drive new cars every year or two, pay the dinner tab for friends, and never seem to "blink" when the news says the stock market is down the toilet.

Back to the reading of my grandmother's will. It was a long reading. I remember the exact words when her will mentioned the new trusts, saying that we should go and "make something of ourselves in this world" and that this money should help us do so.

My grandmother's message was clear and to the point. It was what I needed personally to hear to make sense of how and why this was happening to plain ol' me! And, more than two decades later, those words ring just as loudly. They always come to mind when making big decisions.

My heartfelt message to parents or grandparents preparing a trust: Leave a really clear, simple and positive message to nurture and guide. During those really tough moments we all experience, those crossroads where we have to make a choice to go one way or another and we look for guidance — that's when your simple message will suddenly come back loud and clear.

Don't give a list of rules to lead the recipients to where you want them to go — that can lead to resentment and feelings of being controlled. Life doesn't work the same for everyone and all of us have a path to follow that will lead us where we need to go.

My grandmother's will provided for each of us to receive a lump sum to hold us over until our new trusts were established. My trustee and my attorney told me straight up to save it. They educated me about the stock market, banking, finance, and about trusts — gave me a nice foundation. But did I listen to them? Of course not! Like a good Trustafarian, I made sure the lump sum distribution didn't last long — spending it all within several years.

My trustee had been my mother's trustee as far as I could remember and so I had known his name. He was traditional and professional. He was always eloquent in the way that he spoke, like an English gentleman. Over the years of our working directly with one another, he looked out for my best interests, not just the bank's. He saw me as an individual separate and apart from everyone else and never judged me. He was very patient and supportive while holding me accountable. I felt safe and grounded. He gave me room to "learn through my experiences" and that is exactly what happened. We developed trust that I still have today.

There was always humanity and humor. I sent birthday cards, holiday cards and of course gifts. But, rather than those boring business gifts my mother would send — ties and scarves — I sent the wackiest gifts I could find. One Christmas I gave desktop trains that whistled and traveled on a mini-track. Every afternoon at three, my banker would hit the button on his desktop choo-choo and the loud whistle sound of a train leaving the station would carry throughout the ground floor — letting all know it was time to go home.

I always went back to my attorney and my trustee to ask what they thought of any business endeavor or financial offer. They would always say the same thing: "It's your decision but play it safe. Better safe than sorry, especially with your being so young. You'll need that money when you're older."

My trustee was very forthcoming about the bank wanting to invest my trust fund for longevity. That was the big thing: Longevity, longevity. Every time I spoke with him (it didn't matter what we talked about), the word was: "We want this money to be there for you in your fifties, sixties and seventies." In order to achieve that, the bank invested my funds to grow slowly over time. As painful as it was to see such small numbers in those early days, it was a relief not to have lost everything during the 2008 financial crisis!

My life has had its ups and downs. It took me 20 years to learn the immeasurable difference between being successful through my own efforts versus having money given to me. Today I have a good career and have gone back to school to get a PhD.

People have come in and out of my life for various reasons. A few had financial gain in mind — you learn to see folks like that coming a mile away. The greatest experience has been developing powerful, lasting friendships with people who have never judged me for being a Trustafarian.

In truth, I wouldn't change a day. It was the experience of both my successes and my failures that brought me here and keep me grounded.

Now for some advice to trustees: You are in a position to have a strong influence on the welfare of another individual. Each beneficiary has a distinct personality and a voice that must be heard. Even though we act like a bunch of children from time to time, we are still truly vulnerable. So please, find your own mentor at work, be empathetic, be human and — no matter what — never judge your clients.

And my advice to fellow Trustafarians is to focus on growing up — slowly! The money can be a blessing and a curse. So find and develop strong pillars of support and guidance, meaning a trustee, an attorney, a therapist, a teacher from your school — a "go-to person" who is neutral, objective, and will always be there without crossing the boundary between you.

Don't make important decisions before talking to your go-to person. Utilize their experience and insight until you develop your own.

That, to me, is "growing up."

A poignant story of life as a "Trustafarian." And as we so often hear expressed in different ways, the grandmother's "clear, simple and positive message" has been a constant refrain long after her death. That might be her greatest legacy.

YOU CAN'T TAKE IT PERSONALLY

Occasionally a trustee is paired with someone whose financial wealth seems to be to all they have left. They know how to get along, but hard knocks, combined with bad decisions, have left them personally isolated. What does it take for a trustee to swallow hard, remain available, and become a positive facilitator? (As opposed to what most of the beneficiary's prior relationships turned into.) Here, an institutional trustee is making a difference with a personal approach.

Out of seven siblings, five had committed suicide. Their father, an autocrat, had not been kind to anyone. (I heard the story that he once kicked an IRS agent out of the house — using his foot.) And this family had seen plenty of alcohol abuse.

I dealt with the last surviving sibling, a daughter. She drove a Rolls-Royce, had lots of assets — and was very, very unhappy. Her personal relations with people were not good. In fact, emulating her father, she had become somewhat of an autocrat herself.

And yet — we developed a very good relationship. It took lots of accommodation and, on my part, a thick skin. Sometimes you have people who don't say the nicest things to you and you can't take it personally.

I saw her once per month for probably five or six years. One of the reasons I saw her monthly was to help with her bills. She was losing her eyesight.

She wanted to leave her assets to charitable beneficiaries, and she especially wanted to do something that helped other people who were losing their sight. I did some checking with a certain university and with various eye specialists. I introduced her but she did not get along with them — not at all. So we kept talking about other options.

Eventually, a non-profit in California emerged that fit all the criteria she was talking about. They teach blind people to interact with their guide dogs. Interestingly, she herself did not need a guide dog — she had more eyesight than that.

Along with that organization in California, she ultimately gave her money to one other charity. She did good by doing what she wanted. She also put in her will that she wanted me to have some things. (Of course, I disclaimed.)

Not only did I have a good relationship with her during her life, I was one of two people at her funeral. I didn't have to go — it's just that you develop these relationships and they are close. The fact is, a beneficiary might start looking to you for the type of assistance expected from a friend or a family member, especially when there are none.

Unlike just about everyone else along the trail of this beneficiary's life, our trustee had a single-minded determination to stay focused on the positive. He attributes it to being committed to providing the counsel that is needed, and to having a thick skin. At some point, they began to genuinely like each other. He benefitted, she benefitted, and two charities benefited.

GIVE AND TAKE

Lots of details will be set forth at this story's start, but keep an eye out for the changing of the guard. Uncle chairs the trust from FDR's time all the way to the Nixon years. Storyteller's dad chairs it for the next 20 years. And the storyteller himself takes the helm in 1993. What to notice: The pivotal status of a trust officer over the course of three decades.

My grandfather died in 1936, leaving a will and two codicils. Among the dispositive provisions was a trust set up for his children, their issue, and all of the spouses of the children and issue, as well as certain charitable interests.

My grandfather had three children — my aunt who lived a very private life; my uncle, an eccentric member of the bar; and my father, a college professor. Three different career paths, three very different personalities, three different sets of attitudes regarding the estate — and three personalities who didn't really get along too well. My father had seven children; my uncle, two.

For much of the past 75 years, there have been five trustees. My uncle chaired the trust from the '30s to the early '70s. Then my father became the chairman. In 1993, I became chairman.

One of our trustees has always been a corporate trustee. My grandfather had imagined a stable banking system in which one bank would be the corporate trustee forever. But the banking world became dynamic and fluid. The bank that my grandfather chose became a very troubled institution. Our trust officer moved to another trust company.

We had to make a difficult decision. We didn't yet know how different the banking world would become. But we had greater faith in our trust officer than in the bank he had left; and so, shortly thereafter, we followed him. It seemed a little bit strange at the time, but now, of course, we know that it was absolutely appropriate.

From that point on, we realized that the real basis of our relationship with any corporate trustee was our trust officer. He was the face of the corporate trustee.

Over the years, we followed him several times as he changed institutions. At all times, we knew that he had a really good understanding of our family and its issues. This relationship has been one of about 30 years.

In every situation, our trust officer has been able to size up the people he is dealing with. Based on his ability to find the center of gravity in a meeting or in a room, we would move in the right direction. His presence over the years has helped us to steer a course that has made sense to us as a family and, at the same time, stayed within the expectations of the founding document and the expectations of our state's Attorney General.

Only a few years after I became chairman, a beneficiary felt that the trustees were abusing their discretion. For 10 years, this beneficiary repeatedly took us to court with various complaints. The court upheld the trustees in a series of rulings. The dissident beneficiary continued to threaten further legal action.

Our trust officer had to deal with almost daily correspondence from this one beneficiary. He always responded rationally and unemotionally. With his help, we reached a satisfactory agreement with the dissident beneficiary and the agreement was approved by the court.

He was very good at guiding us even when our course of action was, in a sense, against the interests of the trust company. Just a little bit before I became chairman, we realized that two beneficiaries' individual needs were greater than what could be given to all of the beneficiaries, if we were not to shrink the principal. As trustees, we made a conscious decision to gradually shrink and eventually terminate the trust.

My aunt had never wanted to draw funds from the trust. She admonished our trust officer that this money was a nest egg for her old age and that we should not be talking to her about giving any money to her when she didn't particularly need it.

We promised my aunt that the trust would always be there as a backup for her if she needed it. When we were down to just a couple hundred thousand dollars, we notified her that we were suspending all distributions from the trust to make certain that, in the event that she should need to draw money, it would be available. When my aunt died in her 99th year, we zeroed out the trust, which, of course, eliminated the need for trustees.

There was never a shadow of a doubt during the 30 years that we worked together that — although our trust officer was paid by the trust company — he worked for our family's best interests.

Two more examples: As a result of poor health and a painful divorce, my beautiful sister's life became very difficult. She had some special needs as a beneficiary. She was a trustee along with the corporate trustee, me, and two other individuals.

The trust officer and I came to believe that although there wasn't a legal conflict of interest, we were getting close to an appearance of a conflict because my sister was getting substantially more from the trust than other people within the family. We felt that propriety required she resign as trustee.

We drove to my sister's home to meet with her. The trust officer helped her sort through the idea that, if she stepped down as trustee, it would be easier for us to recognize her needs as a beneficiary. That was difficult for her but she was a logical person. She accepted our advice.

On another occasion, my father had back surgery. Members of the family, along with our trust officer, got together to visit him at the hospital. When staff told us that only family members were permitted to be in the room with my father, we said, "Well, we are all family," and we had our visit.

In addition to his being proactive and calm in the face of conflict, I appreciated our trust officer's friendship and good humor. He was in tune with everyone. He gave us each the opportunity to vent, from time to time, before finding consensus and moving on.

My uncle was a bit of a character. Our trust officer treated his comments and his way of thinking with respect. He told me, "I never got upset. Sometimes it was refreshing to have somebody call and think totally out of the box. He called me one morning and asked, 'Do you think the world will collapse today? Ought we go to gold?' I said, 'No, but I will think about it and give it serious consideration.' I regarded him as somebody who really believed what he said and deserved respect. Five minutes later, he called me and asked if I'd changed my mind. We had another nice conversation."

Our trust officer continued: "If a beneficiary is a little bit unusual, that shouldn't bother someone in my position. I might not always agree, but at the same time it is refreshing that they don't passively accept what I am saying. I enjoy the give and take."

"Almost everyone in this family is educated, articulate," he went on. "They are good people, extraordinarily easy to deal with. You can disagree, you can agree, and everybody remains even-tempered and respectful of everybody else. There are a variety of skills and lifestyles, but everybody gets along. [This storyteller's] father strikes me as one of the most honorable people that I have ever met. I think that carries through with all of his children."

Even after the termination of our family trust, we have maintained a relationship with our trust officer. His company acts as co-trustee and investment advisor for two private foundations. The trust officer and I are contemporaries. Every so often we get together for lunch. That is always a pleasure.

The moral of this story that a trustee's presence can add to the beneficiary's life in ways that continue even beyond the life of the trust. While it is easy to take trustee relationships for granted, or see them as an irritant, it is wise to remember what "best in show" can look and sound like.

LEARNING AND THEN TEACHING

Here's a report of the personal experience of being both a trustee and a beneficiary. The storyteller is, by his own account, "constantly learning and changing," as a vital part of being responsible.

My parents were divorced when I was around 12 years old. My mom remarried. I have a brother and two younger stepsisters. Our wealth is on my dad's side of the family, which led to differences between my early life and that of my stepsisters.

I was introduced to our trust when I was 18. Many beneficiaries don't like trustee involvement. They are not fond of their trustees because they want full control of their inheritance. They feel that they are entitled to everything and need it right now.

But I have never felt that way. The trustees I've had have really taken the time to understand what I'm doing and how I am doing it. When issues come up, we talk. I have them to think with. We work together to find the best way to tackle situations.

Two years ago, I lost my stepdad. He had been very important to us. His was the first death of a close family member that my brother and I experienced.

During this traumatic time, he and I took care of our mom. Even though our trustees had not known her, they listened to what we wanted to accomplish and gave their best advice.

As time went on, we wanted our mom to feel financially independent — to become stable, and support herself.

Our trustees advised us how to help her set up her finances, and also about the human side of things. They suggested we assist her to find her way with the skills she had, and learn new ones as they became necessary. She could always come to us for financial help if she needed.

Our mom has taken steps to create an independent life — something she has never had before. We bought her a house. She has a job and pays the bills. The process has had a positive outcome for her and for us.

I'm glad to have trustees to help with issues like that.

Over the years, I've dealt with a lot of different trustees, financial managers, and advisors. My best education has come from trustees who took time to tell me about the family businesses, how the wealth was made, about family members I did not know who were part of the trust, and about managing wealth.

Sometimes beneficiaries like me want to do things but don't take time to see the best way of going about it. When I was younger, I remember wanting to make quick decisions. It helped to discuss my ideas with a trustee who asked me to slow down and think about it. That made a difference.

Our trustees have good communication skills. They use different approaches to deal with the different personalities in our family. They try to understand us as individuals and help us with what we need. It's been neat to see how the trust can support different types of people, investments, and endeavors.

In recent years I've been a trustee as well as a beneficiary, which has brought me even greater perspective. I'm constantly learning and changing and have a great deal of responsibility. I've been given a lot of good advice about being a wise trustee and providing good counsel.

It can be hard when I really want to see someone's dream succeed, but know that I have to consider my responsibilities to the other beneficiaries, as well. I have to step back and make judgments that are best for the whole.

Guiding younger family members is part of my role as a trustee. I am proud to help them understand what a trustee is, what a beneficiary is, the point of our annual meetings, and what the trust company is and does. I tell them about our family and about my experiences. We talk about what's important to them and what they want to do to earn a livelihood. Knowing about our family and our trust helps them manage their lives more productively.

I am constantly seeking knowledge about how to continue our trust company into the future in much the same way as it is today. I want the next generations to have the services that have helped me so much.

A positive trust relationship "paid forward" is at the core of this story. The storyteller's positive experience as a beneficiary — along with observing, interacting, asking — made it easier to move into his current role.

FAMILY MATTERS

Decades of warm interaction with an uncle lead this storyteller into taking on a family responsibility — becoming a co-trustee — that she otherwise never would've had the training to chance. She grows to understand "the multi-generational family context and the dynamics going on between people and between generations." And we see the value of allowing caring principles, conversation, and sequential deliberation, to work their course.

My own mother died almost 50 years ago. At the time of her death, I was a teenager and the oldest of four. My uncle, whom I will affectionately call "Uncle A," took great interest in our family during my mother's illness and after her death. He came to visit often, and spent holidays with us. He also raised hard-to-talk-about topics, as part of inquiring about our well-being.

This much-adored uncle was really a second father to the four of us. And, upon reaching the age of 90, he began talking to me about his request that I become a co-trustee for his step-granddaughter. Though Uncle A was feeling quite well, he was a planner and — as should be apparent by now — took seriously the long-term welfare of the younger generations in our extended family.

He and his step-granddaughter had had a very scratchy relationship. He asked me to consider taking on the responsibility as a trustee for her. He said that there would be another trustee — an institutional trustee to handle the administration of the trust — but he was very interested in having me guide her.

My long history with this loving and involved uncle would make it hard to say no. But I thought about the request for a long time because the relationship between him and his step-granddaughter was so difficult. It was fraught with upset, with conversations ending in screaming and misunderstanding. Not only that, but she lived on the opposite side of the country from me.

I had three specific concerns. One was that the relationship was getting more problematic between her and Uncle A. I was concerned that she would see me as his "agent" to the point that she and I would not be able to establish a separate relationship.

The second concern was that this young woman, although she had been educated, hadn't been able to launch an independent life and career apart from her mother who was dependent on her.

And the third — and really the most revealing of my personal bias — was that this young woman, whom I did not really know, had many piercings on her face, ears and body. I found it difficult to look at them and wondered how I would relate.

This young woman was trying to find herself. She was getting a Masters degree in history from a fine university and supported herself and her mother, although meagerly. But the deciding factor was my memory and appreciation for my uncle and what he had done when my own mother died. I took on the responsibility.

At 92, Uncle A took ill. Several months later he died, and I became a trustee.

To educate myself, I spent approximately four hours with the institutional trustee. I spent additional time with the lawyer who crafted the documents and who had known Uncle A and his wife. The goal was to get a general idea of what I needed to do. The institutional trustee would take care of the administration of the trust and investment of the funds. I wanted to understand my role as a guide for this young woman.

I scheduled four visits over a three-month period to meet with her. I thought deeply about the outcomes I wanted to accomplish in these early meetings.

The focus of the meetings was to get to know her and for her to know me. I wanted to understand her — what her mother was like, what her other grandparents were like, what her life course had been so far, and the things that she worried about. I talked to her about my uncle and what he had meant to me in the family, what he had done for me when my mother died, and how he had helped my father.

These were very long conversations. They started in the lawyer's office and ended with a meal and a walk. Together we were able to think about the family in context as a way for her to understand where the money came from, why it was important, whom it was important to — and what it represented to her grandmother and for my uncle, who was her step-grandfather.

I gave her trust context, and gave her a place in the history of the family, so she could think about how she was going to take this and use it to move her life forward as part of a large extended family.

In our talks, my uncle became more understandable to her. His view of young people was not positive. Though my uncle was never able to build a kind and gentle relationship with her, he did care deeply about her. She was a part of this family and that was important to him.

Did she come to like him? No, probably not. But I think her perceptions changed somewhat. She understood that, at some level, he had faced his own life problems.

I was candid. I expressed my hesitation about becoming her trustee and my reasons for wanting to do so as well as my concerns. I saw this as an opportunity for following my Uncle A's wishes but I also knew it would take time and effort. And if it wasn't going to work, we would figure that out soon enough.

I think the breakthrough in our relationship came at our first meeting when I was able to neutrally ask her about the piercings — did it hurt, why so many, what did it represent? I was very curious. I think she understood my real interest in her thinking and decision-making.

After our first meeting, she removed her piercing jewelry. At our second meeting, I noticed and wondered about it. She said, "Well, I think maybe it's time that the piercings go." We did not talk about it again.

At the second meeting, she prepared a set of questions about the inheritance and where it came from, how it grew, what it meant, how her dad would benefit, and how and why it had been established.

I included the institutional trust officer in the third and fourth meetings so he could explain what his job was and what she could expect. She had a set of unrealistic expectations that could set the stage for misunderstanding. We discussed tradeoffs such as, "If she only gets X after expecting Y, what could she do?" She discussed the range between what she expected and what she could get.

I think two things happened. One was that she was sitting across from two people who were not judging her nor trying to control her. The second was the fact that she understood that trusts come with legal structures that are important to follow. They weren't personal judgments against her but they were legal and, while there was some latitude, we had to be respectful of the structures often made for tax purposes.

It was during the third and fourth meetings that she began to understand the constraints. I think the experience of having someone help translate what her responsibility was, and what the trust could or could not provide, allowed her a way to look at it as manageable. Her input was important, and she knew that so no one was trying to control her.

Following these meetings, we committed to meet for a weekend twice a year, with phone calls in between. I go there one weekend and she comes here one weekend. We talk about the trust, her life and her plans. I also take part in her quarterly telephone calls with the institutional co-trustee.

I'm not involved in the day-to-day details of her life, but she knows that I care deeply about her. She has many challenges and important decisions to make. I think I can listen and help her think about her alternatives. I can be a translator for the language of the trust, and discuss the interests of the institution and the needs of this young woman. That's a significant role for me.

There have been a couple of disagreements about distributions, but the avenue is open to air them directly without a fight. In one case, we made a decision that she did not want, and in the other we were able to do what she wanted to do.

We have accomplished a lot together. This young woman will use this money thoughtfully, carefully, in most cases.

She probably doesn't like her grandfather any more than she did. And these unresolved issues with her grandfather could have resulted in a difficult relationship with the institutional trustee. To her credit, her understanding changed through the course of our conversations. The institutional trustee will not have to deal with things that were not of its making.

I personally learned about the value to the trust relationship of somebody who understands the multi-generational family context and the dynamics that go on among people and between generations. With that understanding, a trustee has the ability to help the trust function well.

The institutional trustee has done an outstanding job of giving me information and walking alongside of me. I think they also learned that there is real value in understanding the beneficiary in the context of her family.

If I were asked by a trust company for advice, I would suggest that they try new things to keep their thinking fresh. That isn't feasible with all clients, of course, but where you can try to serve as mentor, guide, have an understanding of family — these actions and factors can make a difference. Help beneficiaries think about the money, where it came from, its use, and the conditions under which the trust was structured.

I think there is a great deal to be learned to push your thinking forward. That's a very clear bias of what I think is important — keep learning, keep thinking about it differently, and you will likely provide a more significant service.

As for advice to trust-creators? Learn from my uncle. When he established his trust, he got to know the people at the trust company. He knew the trust officers by name and they knew him. Every time he revised his documents, he personally delivered them to the trust company and got reacquainted with the people there.

And to beneficiaries? Each beneficiary has to ask for information that is broader, deeper and more understandable from his or her trustee — intent of the trust, the constraints, the people involved, the family's history regarding the trusts.

If enough information is not forthcoming, ask often. As in other situations, we don't know what we do not know. And to spend time and energy imagining bad will or other problems where they barely exist does not help anyone.

One final word about why I accepted my Uncle A's request. I've thought a lot about the importance of service to one's family and taking on these responsibilities. How do you do it? What are your principles?

It was, and continues to be, a pleasure for me to give back to the future of the family. That is a value I hold important. I realized that I could try to make a difference in this young woman's life. I didn't want to get bogged down in a troubled relationship, yet I had enough confidence in her and in myself that we could work this out well.

My uncle had been a very important resource for me and I was hoping to do that for his step-granddaughter.

"Uncle A," to use a business term, was a visionary manager: He assembled a duo — two co-trustees with nothing in common but him — to give a fighting chance to a young lady more than six decades his junior. Values and personality clashes did not let him perform the role directly — yet, at age 90, he set up a sound structure. And the niece had enough trust in her uncle to take on a mission that grew less scary with each conversation.

AFTERWORD

The authors thank you for acquiring this book and reading the stories. We hope you got some concrete ideas and are now looking to try a few — to make the move from positive stories to positive steps.

One of the toughest editorial decisions we faced was how much to include about the application to the trustscape of our preferred frameworks: Appreciative inquiry, family systems theory, and positive psychology. The decision? Focus on the stories in *TrustWorthy* and — since we never meant to write a theoretical book — save the in-depth appreciative inquiry/positive psychology/family-systems conversations for NavigatingTheTrustscape.com.

For us, collecting stories is a long-term commitment, with *TrustWorthy* serving as the foundation for a "multi-story" structure. We are continuing to collect stories and make them broadly available on our website. Next time you're there, drop us a note. What worked well for you? What did this book miss? Do you have ideas about where to find the next set of stories?

— Hartley Goldstone and Kathy Wiseman

Hartley Goldstone and Kathy Wiseman are available to deliver a keynote, be on your panel, design a workshop or otherwise address conferences that cover estates & trusts and family dynamics.

NOTES, SOURCES, AND RESOURCES

Jay Hughes' website is JamesEHughes.com — you can read the latest articles by him there. And we highly recommend, if you haven't already done so, picking up a copy of Jay's first book *Family Wealth — Keeping it in the Family* as well as *Family — The Compact Among Generations.*

"John A." Warnick shows the possibility of creating family legacy within the four corners of "purposeful" estate-plan documents. Learn more about John A.'s work by visiting PurposefulPlanningInstitute.com

Jackie Kelm explains the basics of appreciative inquiry in a 10-minute video — see youtube.com/watch?v=ZwGNZ63hj5k

Another excellent resource for appreciative inquiry is AppreciativeInquiry.Case.edu

The family systems theory that that Dr. Murray Bowen built and articulated is available through consultation, DVDs, text, seminars and training at centers and non-profits in Vermont, Massachusetts, Maryland New Jersey, Pennsylvania, Illinois, Kansas, Texas, California, and Florida and. For a full listing, see this web display — TheBowenCenter.org/pages/outsideprograms.html. Kathy Wiseman especially recommends the Bowen Center for the Study of the Family in Washington, DC, and The Learning Space — **(202) 537-5025** — also located in Washington.

Two particularly helpful resources are the Bowen videotape *A Systems View of Human Relationships in the Family, at Work and in Society* and the 1992 book by Dr. Roberta Gilbert, *Extraordinary Relationships*, which is available via Amazon.com.

Positive psychology — the study of optimal human functioning — joins appreciative inquiry to underpin Hartley's work. If you are new to positive psychology, the book *Flourish,* by Dr. Martin Seligman, is a good place to begin.

Over the years, Hartley has found a surprising number of opportunities to learn theory as well as real-world application of positive psychology from professors engaged in leading-edge research as well as noted practitioners. These days he mostly attends courses through MentorCoach.com

Positive psychology researchers have much to say about the correlation between ratios of positive to negative interactions and high performance, life satisfaction and other measures of flourishing. See, for example:

Dr. Marcial Losada (teams) — en.wikipedia.org/wiki/Losada_line

Dr. Barbara Frederickson (individuals) — PositivityRatio.com

Dr. John Gottman (marriages) — youtube.com/watch?v=Xw9SE315GtA

Special thanks go to our editorial advisor and technician Frank Gregorsky of Oakton, Virginia. His website is ExactingEditor.com

And to our designer and publishing consultant, Amy Leigh Campbell, whose website is theHTMelle.com

Made in the USA
Lexington, KY
28 December 2013